Beloved Bride

The Study

What if it's time for the bride to make herself ready
and that bride is YOU?

Rhonda de la Moriniere

To Matthew de la Moriniere,

I stood before you and Jesus and promised to become someone I had no idea how to be. I'm so thankful that we are still here, two very imperfect people, yet still choosing to be held together within His perfect love. Thank-you for all the ways you knowingly and unknowingly are helping to prepare my heart for our heavenly Bridegroom.

SHMILY,

Rhonda

I would like to take an opportunity to acknowledge someone who has been used by God to help me get this book birthed into the world.

Without Brenda Berlingeri, I am not so sure this book would be here today. As a long time member of my first group of Bible study ladies, she fell in love with this study and was the first to insist that I change the name from *One Bride* to *Beloved Bride.* In her words, "we are His Beloved!"

Her calls, texts, and instant messages always arrived just in time, always asking the same question "have you published the book, yet?"

Brenda, your questions were like Christ's whispers to my heart (okay, let's be real, sometimes more like His megaphone). Sometimes loud, yet always convicting, reminding me that, however unknown I am to others, I have a known purpose in our Beloved Bridegroom.

I love you and thank-you for your help in encouraging me and praying for me until this book was ready.

Brenda would want every one of you to know that these words are as real over you as they are to her, *"I am my beloved's, and my beloved is mine; he feedeth his flock among the lilies."(Song of Soloman 6:3)*

Your Beloved Bride Sister Forever,

Rhonda

I also want to acknowledge all my sisters who have faithfully walked beside me as we've journeyed with Him. You have no idea who often your faces, your words, and the many memories of our time together have touched my heart and brought me encouragement to remember Who I'm doing this for and how important it is. I thank you each for being my bridesmaids and allowing me the beautiful privilege of getting to peep at you behind your wedding veils, as you've peeped behind mine. You are truly the MOST BEAUTIFUL brides of all! *"You yourselves are our letter of recommendation, written on our hearts, to be known and read by all." (2 Corinthians 3:2).*

And lastly, I want to acknowledge you, wherever you are, whoever you are, for taking the time to let Jesus, our Beloved Bridegroom, take you by the hand to lead you to the place you most belong, His heart. May you truly encounter His love and His identity over you as His Beloved Bride.

Contents

Introduction vii

Terms and Definitions x

Week 1: A New Name 1

    Day   1 1

    Day   2 6

    Day   3 12

    Day   4 16

    Day   5 21

Week 2: New Name=New Purpose 25

    Day   1 25

    Day   2 31

    Day   3 37

    Day   4 43

    Day   5 50

Week 3:You+Jesus=One 57

    Day   1 57

    Day   2 63

    Day   3 69

    Day   4 76

    Day   5 81

Week 4: Naked and Not Ashamed 87

Day 1 87

Day 2 93

Day 3 98

Day 4 103

Day 5 108

Week 5: Saying Yes to the Dress 113

Day 1 113

Day 2 116

Day 3 119

Day 4 122

Day 5 125

Week 6: Saying Yes to the Dress (Part 2) 129

Day 1 129

Day 2 133

Day 3 137

Day 4 142

Day 5 148

Week 7: The Covering 152

Day 1 152

Day 2 159

Day 3 168

Day 4 176

Day 5 184

Introduction

"And I will betroth you to me forever. I will betroth you to me in righteousness and in justice, in steadfast love and in mercy. I will betroth you to me in faithfulness. And you shall know the LORD." (Hosea 2:19-20)

We are about to walk through a life changing journey together, one that will change the way you see yourself, purpose, and the world around you. Before you were born, Jesus looked upon you and whispered these words over you, "you shall know the Lord." Against the dark backdrop of this world, He's laid out a scarlet trail, the wedding aisle of His love for you, upon which He invites you to rise and shine and know that He is both your Lord and Bridegroom.

We will discover how this marriage took place as we walk through each step of an ancient Hebrew wedding. We will not only witness how Jesus fulfilled each one, but also take time to absorb these moments, making them personal to each of our individual lives. You will discover your own love story with the Savior as you see Him through the rightful lens of your beloved Bridegroom, who has and is already carrying the weight of your life across the threshold of this earthly experience. You will discover Him to be the most faithful Bridegroom.

This study has changed my life more than any other has. It has changed the way I see eternity, which has changed the way I see my marriage, my mothering, and each moment of my existence. I know it will do the same for you as you discover your identity and begin to live as the bride of Christ. At one time in my life, my experiences in this world seemed so big and real, even bigger, and more real than Jesus. Yet, as He began to reveal Himself to me through the lens of the Bridegroom, He became the substance I lived in, eclipsing every other earthly experience in His shadow.

We live in a world where a covenant or promise means very little. So much so, that it may harden our hearts towards believing that even God can keep His promise to us.

Yet, as we look to Jesus, and see that He not only kept His covenant promise to us but is keeping it still. In Him, we have a sure place to stand beneath our feet, and as we contemplate our role as His bride, we will find ourselves standing in this place too.

Too often, we trust Jesus for salvation and then begin to journey along a weighty path of following our own expectations of who we are in Him. After all, we made a promise and now we must keep it, right?

We confuse trusting our promises to Jesus with trusting His promise to us. Until, after countless tries to follow Him, we began to sink under the weight of it all and either start pretending, performing, or walk away completely

As we will discover through this journey together, being His bride has never been about what we do, it's always been about who we have become because of all He's done.

As He expresses in Hosea 2:19-20, *"And I will betroth you to me forever. I will betroth you to me in righteousness and in justice, in steadfast love and in mercy. I will betroth you to me in faithfulness. And you shall know the LORD."*

The weight of our journey has already fallen upon His shoulders, and we get to spend our lives allowing Him to carry us through the beauty and wonder of who we truly become once we became His.

We will begin with a wedding itinerary, which will include Hebrew terms that are important for our study.

Each week's study will begin with taking one more step down our ancient Hebrew wedding aisle, as we examine both the ancient Hebrew cultural portion of the ceremony as well as how Jesus fulfilled it and is fulfilling it in our lives.

There is a book that encapsulates the weekly teachings that coordinate with this study available, that can help make these moments more personal to your own life as you allow your heart to interact with what you are learning about Jesus' marriage to you. I strongly encourage you to read this weekly Bible study along with the book as they are intended to go together to help you fully enter your experience as the bride of Christ. Remember, this journey is about understanding who you've become as Christ's bride. The study portion allow you that opportunity.

I encourage you to take your time and enjoy your walk down the wedding aisle with Jesus. Give yourself time to **see** the beauty of who you've become through His grace. Revelation 19:7 says, *"Let us exalt and give him glory, for the marriage of the Lamb has come, and His Bride has made herself ready."* There comes a time for every bride when she must look in the mirror as she is and prepare herself for who she's becoming as His bride.

This is your moment.

Welcome, beloved bride.

Terms and Definitions

B'rit: covenant (sealed in blood), Old Testament

B'rit Hadashah: New Covenant, Tanakh, sealed in Christ's blood

Kidushin: Betrothal period (think of Mary and Joseph), this is the name given for the period of time after the 1ˢᵗ part of the wedding takes place as the bride waits for the second part to begin. It usually lasts anywhere from one to two years; however, no one knows when the second part will begin except the groom's father. The father watches over the son as he builds the dwelling place for his bride and the father determines when that dwelling is ready and complete as he announces to his son, "Go get your bride," once his desired completion for the dwelling is finished by his son.

Da'at: I do, the bride has the ability to give her consent or reject the wedding proposal. Her father calls her and asks for her consent as the father of the groom and his son approaches the father of the bride to ask for her hand. The Holy Spirit calls for us and asks for our consent. To accept or reject the wedding proposal is up to the bride. Should she consent, she gives her Da'at, her "I do" and seals this by sharing a cup with her bridegroom.

Ketubah: wedding contract. This is presented to the bride on her wedding day and signed at the second part of the wedding by the bride. It is the bridegroom's covenant to his bride, displaying all the promise he intends to her as well as his assuming full responsibility for her body, soul and spirit. All of who she is will be transferred to his shoulders should she accept his covenant promise to her. Our Ketubah is God's Word, His new covenant to us as written in the New Testament.

Mohar: Bride Price. This is what it cost the bridegroom's father to purchase the bride. It is indicative of the value the father and son saw in the bride. Our Mohar is the blood of

Christ, the Father's Son. It was the highest price paid, for the Father sees the true value in each of us.

Ka'lal: Bride or "set apart one." Once sealed during the first portion of the wedding ceremony, the bride wears a veil over her face in public as a demonstration that she has been "set apart" for betrothal. We are "set apart" in Christ, sealed through His Holy Spirit through Whom we are able to demonstrate to the world that we are taken and betrothed to Christ, sealed for His glory.

Mikvah: Hebrew for baptism (more precisely, immersion). This is the bride's time for beautification. Jewish family tradition states that a woman is to re-do this each month after her cycle, as she becomes "new" again for her husband. The bride is to be fully submerged in a living body of water, symbolizing her new birth. Her first mikvah takes place before the second portion of the wedding begins. Our mikvah is our baptism as we are washed away from our old life and cleansed and made new in Christ. He also washes us in His Word throughout our journey with Him. He is our Living Water as we walk beside Him as His bride.

Chadar (Kadar): wedding chamber. This is presented in the second portion of the wedding. It is the bride's house that the bridegroom has added on to his father's house. It is what he was building while his wife was in her time of preparation and waiting. Jesus is working on this right now as He is building His church (Bride), while at the same time in heaven building a literal place for us to dwell eternally with Him.

Aperion: The bridal litter. This was a special carriage that was prepared for the bride, carried on the backs of groomsman, it transported the bride to her awaiting bridegroom at the call of the groom's father as the second portion of the wedding begins. She literally meets her groom in the air. For us, this gives reference to the rapture of Christ's church, His Bride.

The Huppah: The original meaning is room or covering. It is where the bride and groom will enter to consummate their marriage and where they will stay for seven days as they "yada" (get to know one another intimately) for the first time. Perhaps this is where we will spend seven years with our Bridegroom/ King just after the rapture as we finally get to know Him face to face.

Week 1:
A New Name

DAY   1

"Jacob went on his way, and the angel of God met him. And when Jacob saw them he said, 'This is God's camp!' So he called the name of the place Mahanaim." (Genesis 32:1-2)

"Then the LORD said to Moses, Tell the people of Israel to turn back and encamp in front of Pi-hahiroth, between Migdol and the sea, in front of Baal-zephon; you shall encamp facing it, by the sea." (Exodus 14:1-2)

We learned this week what the word Mahanaim means, God's camp on earth.

Please, take a moment and write your name in the statement below.

_______________________ *is God's camp on earth.*

What does the words above mean to you? What does it mean to be God's camp on earth?

____

____

____

____

____

First, I don't know about you, but outside of smores, I HATE camping! In fact, the very mention of the word fills my mind with memories of stuffy tents, smelly, wet sneakers, the scent of bug spray mixed with the sting of smoke in my eyes. Perhaps, even worse are the complications that arise when we must go without our modern conveniences, such as a restroom. During our last camping trip, our site was nearly a half-mile from the nearest bathroom. To make matters worse, we were staying near the water, which meant there were no trees to take cover in should an "emergency" arise.

My anxiety over my distance from the restroom did not afford me any rest. Nope, camping is not a restful experience …at least for this suburb mom.

Considering the above description of my love for camping, I bet you won't be surprised to find out that I have **never** once initiated a camping trip. Any camping trip I have ever been on, was not my idea. Camping is just **not** my idea of a vacation.

In Genesis 32:1-2, it states that Jacob was, "on his way," what made him name the place he was standing, God's camp?

____

____

____

____

____

Would you say Jacob was initiating this encounter or responding to it? Explain

____

____

____

____

____

In Exodus 14:1-2, who is planning this first "camping trip" for the Israelites?

____

____

____

____

____

In verses 3-4, God tells Moses, *"For Pharaoh will say of the people of Israel, 'They are wandering in the land; the wilderness has shut them in.' And I will harden Pharaoh's heart, and he will pursue them, and I will get the glory over Pharaoh and all his host, and the Egyptians shall know that I am the LORD. And they did so."*

Beloved, you may not understand this "camping" trip that you are on, you may even feel like turning around and heading back to Egypt more times than you care to mention. However, one of the very first steps in becoming who we are meant to be as Christ's bride is to know WHO has initiated this whole thing.

I have known many women who have felt forced into marriage, whether it is through an unplanned pregnancy, or an inability to own one's boundaries before entering into that covenant agreement, or just plain insecurity that caused her to manipulate herself into a wedding band. Whatever the case has been, there are times later in the marriage where she will doubt herself, her marriage, and her husband. She will often wonder, "did he marry me because he **had** to, or because he **wanted** to?" I can assure you beloved, Jesus **wanted** to marry you. Perfect love, the only perfect Man that exists in all creation looked at you and decided that He would rather die than to live without you.

You are His Beloved, His camp on earth. However hard, whatever it takes, He will never stop loving you.

In Revelation 21:6, Jesus says, *"It is done! I am the Alpha and the Omega, the beginning and the end."* As we saw earlier in our study, Jesus is the initiator of this relationship with you. And as hard as this camping trip may become at times, He is also the conclusion of it, the beginning and the end. He is *your* beginning and your end.

Let's take a moment to affirm this truth, write your name in the blank space below

JESUS ____ **JESUS**

Not long ago I was very ill. In truth, I was so ill that there were times when no one (including me) knew if I would survive. This was a huge time of testing for me. There were times when I became so anxious and afraid. One instance I remember crying out to the Lord and asking Him to prepare me for what was to come. If I were going to die, I wanted to know and to become ready. I would throw His word back up to Him, "Jesus, You said that You would be a lamp unto my feet and a light to my path!" And then I would yell out my list of how all the things that I was experiencing led to my uncertainty. I felt very much like I was in the dark. I will never forget the morning when He confronted me about this. He reminded me about His words in Deuteronomy 30:19-20, *"I call heaven and earth to witness against you today, that I have set before you life and death, blessing and curse. Therefore, choose life that you and your offspring may live, loving the LORD your God, obeying His voice and holding fast to Him, for He is your life and length of days…"*

 I knew at that moment what He was saying to me, "Rhonda, why do you concern yourself with whether you will live or die? The questions that you are asking were already answered the minute you gave your heart to Me. You will live Rhonda. What is it to you if your earthly life ends next week or 100 years from now? You are Mine! I am your life and your length of days so no matter what happens on earth, I have already secured a "happy ending" for you."

*Is there any area in your life where Jesus may be asking you to choose **life** right now? Explain.*

____

____

____

____

____

____

And, no matter what you are facing right now, He has already secured a happy ending for you.

Let's close by writing a prayer of thanks to our Beloved for beginning this journey with us and securing a happy ending for us.

DAY 2

"And the messengers returned to Jacob saying, "We came to your brother Esau, and he is coming to meet you, and there are four hundred men with him." Then Jacob was greatly afraid and distressed. He divided the people who were with him, and the flocks and herds and camels, into two camps, thinking, "If Esau comes to one camp and attacks it, then the camp that is left will escape." (Genesis 32:6-8)

"For we know that if the tent, which is our earthly home, is destroyed, we have a building from God, a house not made with hands, eternal in the heavens. For in this tent we groan, longing to put on our heavenly dwelling." (2 Corinthians 5:1-2)

I am reading a book on marriage right now, and last night I came across a comment that really intrigued me. The comment is from the book, Boundaries in Marriage, and it reads, "you must become a complete individual on your own in order to have true oneness with your spouse." (Cloud and Townsend, 1999). I laughed as I read the comment above and thought to myself, "how in the world does one become *complete* on their own?" If I had waited until I was complete to marry my husband, I would have never married. It has taken marriage to point out to me, like a beaming spotlight, all my areas of incompleteness.

Like Jacob on his way to face the fears of his past, we sometimes need "messengers" to come and tell us where we stand in our journey. And like Jacob, once they come, we often become greatly distressed and divided.

What has been your greatest journey through fear so far in your life? How did you respond to it?

____

____

____

____

____

It is ironic that in our human nature, when faced with the most challenging times in our lives, instead of standing in solidarity, we often instead choose to split in weakness. Like Jacob, perhaps we perceive that if we can escape with a little, it is better than losing everything. So often in our relationships, we respond out of our fractures instead of our fullness in Christ.

Counselors will say that if two people who are not whole marry, they seek to complete one another. Therefore, creating stunted growth in both persons.

What does Colossians 2:9-10 say? Please, record the scripture below.

____

____

____

____

____

I love how New King James Version states it, *"For in Him dwells all the fullness of the Godhead bodily; and you are **complete** in Him, who is the head of all principality and power"* (the emphasis is mine).

Considering this scripture, beloved, where is your completeness found?

____

____

____

____

____

I will never forget the first time these words really struck my heart. I was working out at the gym and had brought my scripture memory cards with me to review while I was working out. As a victim of childhood abuse, I have had to go through so much healing. I had just spent that morning praying and asking the Lord if I could ever be whole after all I had been through. It just seemed hopeless at times, and I was feeling discouraged. For some reason these words came alive to me at the gym and as God so often does in His Word, it cut through me like a double-edged sword. I remember saying out loud, "you mean I can be whole and complete, God?" And I heard His voice reply, "If you want to." All this time, those words had been there, and He was only waiting for me to believe them and to allow the Truth of His completeness to cover the fractured and broken truth of my past.

Is there a part of you (past or present} that feels fractured right now? Explain.

____

____

____

____

____

In what ways might Jesus be asking you to exchange your fracture for His wholeness?

____

____

____

____

____

We can spend our lives striving to become whole or we can surrender our search to the One Who already made us whole. Sometimes it takes seeing our fractures and letting them break our hearts before we are ready to make the exchange that will heal them.

Beloved, this is a camping trip, it's difficult, beautiful, and yet temporary.

How do you define camping?

____

____

____

____

____

This place may feel like home, but it is not our home.

Look up the following verses and record what they say about our "real" home.

John 14:2-3

____

____

____

____

____

John 14:23

____

____

____

____

____

2 Corinthians 5:6

____

____

____

____

____

Let's read 2 Corinthians 5:1-2 *"For we know that if the tent, which is our earthly home, is destroyed, we have a building from God, a house not made with hands, eternal in the heavens. For in this tent we groan, longing to put on our heavenly dwelling"*

What word is used to describe our earthly bodies?

____

____

____

____

____

In your own words, describe what a tent is.

____

____

____

____

You, beloved, were created to be indwelt by the Spirit of the living God!

As much as I do not enjoy camping, there is something so precious about the image of Jesus walking around our campsite, not only guarding the site from any harm, but peeping into each tent, lifting the face of each one inside, initiating intimate conversations, the kind that are most meaningful and most beautiful while shared near a crackling campfire.

Is there something in your heart you wish you could talk to Him about right now? If so, why not set this study aside and open your heart to Him?

____

____

____

____

____

This is what you were created for, sweet one! You were created for Jesus. Your tent, your body, aches to be indwelt by Life Himself. And if we allow ourselves to become at home in this world, we will begin to feel the fractures of it. However, Christ has invited you to live in a place with Him where there is wholeness, the only true place that it exists in this world.

Remember this quote, "you must become a complete individual on your own in order to have true oneness with your spouse." (Cloud and Townsend,1999). Only Christ can take a fractured heart and exchange it for a whole one. And until we belong to Him, we are not truly able to fully belong to anyone.

DAY 3

"And the messengers returned to Jacob, saying, "We came to your brother Esau, and he is coming to meet you, and there are four hundred men with him." (Genesis 32:6)

"The Egyptians pursued them, all Pharaoh's horses and chariots and his horsemen, and his army, and overtook them encamped at the sea, by Pi-hahiroth, in front of Baalzephon." (Exodus 14:9)

I got up this morning determined to have a wonderful day. I had a wonderful quiet time, great coffee, cool weather, and nice cozy robe. I was determined to not let the hustle and bustle that was about to take place when everyone woke up challenge me. I was going to stay in the joy of the Lord, no matter what!

That all changed when, within a 30-minute window of time, our puppy had three accidents in the house, glass from a bottle of special barbeque sauce broke and cut one of my girls on her leg, my son began hounding me about some things I had not taken care of for him, I burned the eggs I was trying to cook for breakfast, and could not find the leggings that my daughter was insisting on wearing to school. It didn't take long for my plans for a "wonderful day" to dwindle down to desperate prayers of "Jesus, just please help me survive today!"

Just like we saw from our lesson this week, we can start off on "our way", but it doesn't take long for us to realize that we need some "angels of the Lord" to meet us because we need some **help**.

The first mentions of the word "camp" in Scripture is found in Exodus 14:2 and in verse 9 where it says, *"The Egyptians pursued them, all Pharaoh's horses and chariots and his horsemen, and his army, and overtook them encamped at the sea, by Pi-hahiroth, in front of Baalzephon."*

I love it that here we see the word "camp" mentioned in association with the Israelite's freedom. They had just left Egypt, where they had been slaves for more than 400 years. Before they even had the chance to experience what "freedom" felt like, here comes Pharaoh with all his army!

Look up Exodus 14:10-12, how did the Israelites respond when they saw this great army coming towards them?

____

____

____

____

____

When was the last time you felt as if a whole army was coming to overtake you?

____

____

____

____

____

How did you respond?

____

____

____

____

____

"Is it because there are no graves in Egypt that you have taken us away to die in the wilderness? What have you done to us in bringing us out of Egypt?" (Exodus 14:11)

Have you ever felt baffled by the path God has chosen for you? Explain

____

____

____

____

____

One of the hardest parts about following Christ, in my opinion, is knowing that I will never fully arrive at my destination while in the flesh. Just when I think I have 'arrived' at one victory, I seem to be headed out to another battlefield.

However, I take great comfort in knowing that, although I will not arrive at my final home until this earthly life is over, God has chosen to call me His *Mahanaim*, His camp on earth. The greatest part of my everlasting destination is already here! Jesus is camping with each of us through this whole journey!

What about you, what has been the hardest part of following Christ?

____

____

____

____

____

Has there been a time you felt like you would rather go back to Egypt than face another day headed towards the promised land?

____

____

____

____

____

So often, just like the Israelites, we get overwhelmed when trying to live in the freedom that Christ has given us. Just as soon as we become free, it seems as if a whole army is coming towards us to "kill us in the wilderness."

Perhaps, we are like Jacob and the Israelites who fall into despair when we see our captors coming for us, when we hear the wheels of the chariots that threaten to overtake us, and when we feel the same terror that we have associated with these sights and sounds. We tend to panic when threatened.

God did not waste any time in showing the Israelites, or Jacob whose responsibility it was to fight against any threat to His people. Before the Israelites could even begin to celebrate their newfound freedom, God orchestrated one of the greatest displays of His amazing ability to watch over and protect His own through the crossing of the Red Sea.

Read Genesis 32:13-31 and record any special insights below

____

____

____

____

____

We will *camp* the rest of the week in these verses. Just as God initiated a divine wrestling match with Jacob, and just as He led the Israelites on a 40 year long "wrestling match" through the wilderness of their own hearts, He will never stop wrestling against anything that stands in the way of our identity in Him. Remember, He began this camping trip with you, and He will see you through to the end. For, this camping trip life has more to do with discovering Who has become our home than in arriving there. *"For in him we live and move and have our being..." (Acts 17:28).*

DAY 4

"And you shall say, moreover, your servant Jacob is behind us." For He thought, "I may appease him with the present that goes ahead of me, and afterward I shall see his face. Perhaps he will accept me." (Genesis 32:20)

"Will the LORD be pleased with thousands of rams, with ten thousands of rivers of oil? Shall I give my firstborn for my transgression, the fruit of my body for the sin of my soul? He has told you, O man, what is good; and what does the LORD require of you, but to do justice, and to love kindness, and to walk humbly with your God?" (Micah 6:7-8)

I will never forget the sleepless night I spent before my wedding day. Talk about a wrestling match! If anything, we might expect a bride to be sleepless due to the nervous excitement of a new life. However, the nerves I experienced were not due to excitement, they were due to fear! I had been a single mom, a divorced mom of two, and had enough baggage to start my own UPS company. And I was about to marry a man who grew up in the perfect family, with the perfect track record, no baggage that I could see, and no ex-wife and kids. What in the world did he see in me? I knew what I was, and I also knew I had no idea how to become who I was going to need to become for this work out well.

I find so much comfort in scripture, especially my ability to relate to such patriarchs as Jacob, a man who wrestled with God. Like Jacob sending the gifts ahead of him to try and appease what laid behind him (his deception of his brother), I had put my best foot forward, trusting in this relationship, hoping and praying that Jesus truly would cover over all of my past.

The Hebrew definition for the word "appease" used here means to cover his face, or to cover one's guilt. Jacob was sending the gifts ahead of him in hopes that his brother might accept the gifts and relent exacting revenge on him.

We often do the same. So often I find myself treating my children to ice cream, or a trip to some fun place after being in a grumpy mood. Or how about starting a diet on Monday after a weekend binge on junk food? There are countless ways we each try to "cover our face" when we have a guilty conscience.

What are some ways you tend to "cover your face" when you have a guilty conscience?

____

____

____

____

____

So often we use our "covers" to try and appease God. I know many people who felt condemnation regarding sexual sin before they were married. They felt that marriage would "cover" that sin. Also, like me, there have been women who have the sin of abortion in their past, who felt that having children would "cover" that past sin.

What are some other ways that we use our "covers" to try and appease God?

____

____

____

____

____

Reflect again on the verse below...

"And you shall say, moreover, your servant Jacob is behind us." For He thought, "I may appease him with the present that goes ahead of me, and afterward I shall see his face. Perhaps he will accept me." (Genesis 32:20)

Jacob was sending his valuable possession "ahead of him" to try and appease his brother. *In your own life, what do you see as valuable about yourself?*

____

____

____

____

____

In what ways might you try and use these traits or possessions to "go before you?"

____

____

____

____

____

So often we equate God with man. Man so often judges others based on what he sees as value in himself. However, God is not man. 1 Samuel 16:7 says, *"For the LORD sees not as man sees; man looks at the outward appearance, but the LORD looks at the heart."*

So often we don't even take the time to examine what is in our own hearts, nor the hearts of others. However, God knows us, *intimately* knows us. There is never a moment when He judges us based on what we place before us, or behind us. He is always aware of exactly what is going on in our heart. And that is where He waits for us.

If you could name your camp right now based on what is going on in your heart, what would it be called?

____

____

____

____

____

"Will the LORD be pleased with thousands of rams, with ten thousands of rivers of oil? Shall I give my firstborn for my transgression, the fruit of my body for the sin of my soul? He has told you, O man, what is good; and what does the LORD require of you, but to do justice, and to love kindness, and to walk humbly with your God?" (Micah 6:7-8)

Based on the verse above, what does the Lord require of us?

____

____

____

____

____

What offerings (or covers) are mentioned that He does not require of us?

____

____

____

____

____

Which seems easier to give? What He requires or what we think He requires?

____

____

____

____

____

Why is it so difficult to give to God what He actually requires? What does that say about us?

____

____

____

____

I mentioned at the beginning of our lesson today that I was terrified the night before my wedding. I knew what I was, and I knew that I did not have what it takes to make the marriage work out. I will never forget the flood of relief that washed over me the minute I finally spoke those two words, "I do." It was a moment of surrender. By faith, I stood before the man that I love, knowing I did not have what it takes to be his wife. My "do" was based on the One, my beloved Jesus, who had already "done" all that was required for me to become all I would ever need in this life.

*"When Jesus had received the sour wine, he said, "**It is finished**," and he bowed his head and gave up His spirit." (John 19:30)*

As we close, is there any "do" in your life that you would like to exchange for Christ's "done" at the Cross? Why not take this moment and record a prayer of surrender?

DAY   5

"Then he said, "Let me go, for the day has broken." But Jacob said, "I will not let you go unless you bless me. And he said to him, "What is your name?" And he said, "Jacob." (Genesis 32:26-27)

"So Jacob called the name of this place Peniel, saying, For I have seen God face to face, and yet my life has been delivered." (Genesis 32:30)

Yesterday we talked about how we, along with Jacob, try to provide coverings for our face to go before us when we have a guilty conscience. Today, we will discover what happens when those coverings are wrestled off us, and we must stand face to face before God. For some of us brides, it takes a wrestling match with Christ to remove the old name, so that He can make us ready to wear our new one.

Look back over Genesis 32:22-33. Record any new insights or questions below.

____

____

____

____

____

You may find yourself wondering, "who was that masked man?" However, we find in Genesis 32:30 that Jacob names the place where this wrestling match occurred after who he was wrestling with; *"I have seen God face to face."* Many Bible scholars assume that this man was a theophany; a visible (and in this case tangible) manifestation of God.

As we investigate what is occurring here, I find three remarkable things and how it might apply to our lives.

1. We know that God is much stronger than man, but we see here that God is accommodating to Jacob's weakness as they wrestle it out. Psalm 103:14 says, *"He knows our frame, He remembers that we are dust."* How precious it is that God understands our weakness, and even gets down to wrestle with us over our struggles. We don't have to be afraid to bring our doubts to Him. Unlike man, who often attacks when confronted, God will allow us to wrestle it out with Him. He will never let go of us.

    When was the last time you had something you felt you needed to "wrestle" with God about? Did you feel that you had the freedom to do so? Please, share below.

    ____

    ____

    ____

    ____

    ____

    How does it feel knowing there is freedom to wrestle? Explain

    ____

    ____

    ____

    ____

2. In this scene, we see God allowing Jacob to take some ownership and responsibility. We know that God is our ultimate authority, yet the theophany asks Jacob to let go of Him. Jacob replies, *"I will not let you go unless you bless me."* We also see this when the theophany asks Jacob for his name. The name Jacob means deceiver. His name was best personified when he deceived his brother, Esau, whom he must now face. Perhaps it is when Jacob is asked to let go, that he realizes the need to resolve his deceitful nature.

Has there been a time in your life when you could not go one more step forward in your own skin? If so, please share below

____

____

____

____

____

So often we are waiting on a blessing from God, however in this scene we see that Jacob is the one asking for the blessing.

What are your thoughts about the relationship between God's blessings for us and our initiative in receiving the blessing?

____

____

____

____

____

3. The third intriguing aspect of this encounter has to do with Jacob's victory. Perhaps the most precious part in this scene takes place when Jacob finally takes responsibility for his name. His hip is out of socket, he is probably physically and emotionally exhausted from wrestling all night. Yet, we see this beautiful moment when the theophany leans over Jacob and says, *"Your name shall no longer be called Jacob, but Israel, for you have striven with God and with men, and have prevailed"* vs. 28. In our human nature, one gains victory through the defeat of another. However, with Christ, it is in letting go of our own defeated identity that we are able to wear His victory.

Not until we are ready to let go of our "self" are we truly able to accept the fullness of Who Christ is.

What about you beloved, do you feel that you have ever truly admitted the whole truth about yourself to Christ? If so, please, share it below. If not, use this time and space to ask Him to help you.

———————————————————————————————

———————————————————————————————

———————————————————————————————

———————————————————————————————

———————————————————————————————

Beloved, we began this week's journey with an understanding that we are eternal creatures, on a camping trip through this earthly experience.

Before we can go further into this wedding ceremony, where we will truly understand our Oneness with Christ, we must first take responsibility for where we have been in our "self". In early times, one's camp meant more than just where they stayed. It was a place of identity. Your camp represented your people, your tribe. The first step in fully understanding who you are as Christ's bride is to acknowledge where you are, whose camp you have belong to. Romans 5:12 says, "*Therefore, just as sin came into the world through one man and death through sin, and so death spread to all men because all sinned.*" Before Christ our tribe was sin.

Let's reflect on this quote from our lesson in day 2, "you must become a complete individual on your own in order to have true oneness with your spouse." (Cloud and Townsend, 1999).

The very first marriage was officiated by God when He married His crown of creation and, in doing so, created the covenant of marriage. It takes place in Genesis 2:24, "*Therefore a man shall leave his father and mother and hold fast to his wife, and they shall become one flesh.*" Perhaps, Cloud and Townsend were right after all. "You must become a complete individual on your own in order to have true oneness with your spouse." Beloved, before you can fully embrace all that you are in Christ, you must first surrender all of yourself to Him. "*And the two shall become one flesh.*"

Week 2:
New Name=New Purpose

DAY 1

"Wives submit to your own husbands, as to the Lord. For the husband is the head of the wife even as Christ is the head of the church, his body, and is Himself its Savior. Now, as the church submits to Christ, so also wives should submit in everything to their husbands." (Ephesians 5:22-24)

"To the woman he said, "I will surely multiply your pain in childbearing; in pain you shall bring forth children. Your desire shall be for your husband, and he shall rule over you." (Genesis 3:16)

In our lesson this week, we discussed what happens during the first phase in an ancient Hebrew wedding. And we compared how these formalities relate to our wedding to Christ, how during His brief life here on earth, He initiated this wedding proposal to each of us. Our eyes have been opened to a new realm of relationship to Him that we may not have considered before.

This week we will have the opportunity to examine more thoroughly what this means to us. As we mentioned last week, when most of us came to Christ, we became something that we had no idea how to "be". However, as we look closely into the new roles that a Hebrew bride takes on once she is betrothed, new ways of seeing our "how to be" will become clear to us. Although Jesus is ultimately our Way and has planned very distinct and individual purposes for each of our lives here, there are certain responsibilities we are all to fulfill as the Beloved bride of Christ.

If there were one word to sum up what our new role is as a bride, it would be the word, **realize**. The verb realize is defined by Merriam Webster as: *to understand or become aware of, to cause (something) to become real, to achieve (something, such as a goal, dream, etc..)*

Let's make this personal, in view of the above definition, write out your primary role as Christ's bride below

____

____

____

____

____

Let's take a closer look at Ephesians 5:22-24, "*Wives, submit to your own husbands, as to the Lord. For the husband is the head of the wife even as Christ is the head of the church, his body, and is Himself its Savior. Now, as the church submits to Christ, so also wives should submit in everything to their husbands.*"

The Greek word for "submit "used in verse 22 is *Naarah*. It is a word used to describe a female child, or servant. The Greek word in verse 24 is different. It is *Hupotasso*. It means, to subordinate, to obey, to put under, to subdue.

Whether we are married or not, the verses above speak a great deal to us about God's set alignment. So many women in and outside of the church are put off by the word submit. However, as we look closely into this relationship that exists between God, men, and women, we will see something beautiful and amazing within His creation of order.

First, using the above verses and definitions, label the diagram below based on God's pre-scribed order, keeping in mind that the higher the authority, the greater the responsibility.

____

____

____

Many women today want the authority, but not the responsibility. Ask them why they disregard man's authority, and they will likely say it's due to his lack of responsibility. We, as women will often use men's propensity to misalign himself under God as an excuse to misalign ourselves. We forget that God is a God of order. We can't try and obey Him while disregarding His prescribed order at the same time. Staying in His pre-scribed order is, perhaps, a woman's greatest responsibility and challenge in following Christ.

This goes all the way back to the original sin. Let's look back at what happened in Gen-esis 3. Meet me there and let's read verses 1-6 together. Record any insights that stand out to you below.

____

____

____

____

____

Using these verses and the diagram below, fill in the blanks according to the alignment we see taking place. Who followed whose instructions? Compare it to the diagram above, how do they differ?

____

____

____

The enemy, knowing fully well how to deceive the woman, led her out of her alignment. Tempted to become like God, she instead submitted herself to a whole different authority; one of a deceiver.

Based on your perception of how the world is operating right now, draw a diagram to show what your opinion of this world's alignment is

I wish I could see your diagram. It is a difficult concept to consider. I felt like scribbling all over the page. This world seems to be in chaos, there seem to be no straight lines at all. Perhaps, just as he did in the Fall; the enemy has not changed his approach much. Keeping us out of alignment ensures chaos and deception.

What do the following verses say about who now has authority over this world?

John 12:31

____

____

____

____

____

John 14:30

____

____

____

____

____

2 Corinthians 4:4

____

____

____

____

____

Now, let's look at what happened after the Fall. Meet me back in Genesis 3 and let's read verses 7-19 together. Record any new insights below.

____

____

____

____

____

"To the woman he said, "I will surely multiply your pain in childbearing; in pain you shall bring forth children. Your desire shall be for your husband, and he shall rule over you." (Genesis 3:16)

Look at the above verse and compare it to the 2 curses handed (one to the serpent, and the other to Adam). Fill in the blanks below based on who and what is cursed.

In verse 14, who is cursed _____________________?

In verse 16, look closely, is there a mention of the word curse? _____________

Instead of a curse, we see that two aspects of her life will be affected due to her sin; they involve her role as ________________, and ________________.

In verses 17, what is cursed________________________?

As we look at the verses above in light of these new observations, we see the only one who is actually cursed is the serpent. We also see a curse handed to Adam, but it is not to his person, but to the ground, of which his calling and purpose is derived.

One of the sweetest moments occurs just after this horrible time of reckoning. We have all heard the saying; "it is always darkest just before the dawn." Perhaps, this is where that saying originated. It is found in Genesis 3:20. Record below what takes place in this verse.

____

____

____

____

____

The name Eve means the mother of all living. She was given her classification as woman in her creation, which also referenced her calling and purpose as man's helper and companion (refer to Genesis 2:22). But here we see that she is given her name and her redemptive purpose, Eve, mother of all living. We see here the first mention of hope, the very first reference to a turning around of all that had been made wrong. We see the birth of **redemption** associated with Eve.

Just as she represented the bride of Adam, the one who was needed for God's perfect reflection of marriage to take place, and just as she was to become the mother of all living, even in the midst of devastation. So, we become the mother of all living through Christ's death on the Cross. Just as Eve found her purpose and her name just after the darkest moment had passed, so it is with us. As Christ died during the darkest hour this world has ever known, the church, His beloved bride was finally realized, her purpose and her name were born.

DAY 2

"Husbands, love your wives, as Christ loved the church and gave himself up for her, that he might sanctify her, having cleansed her by the washing of water with the word." (Ephesians 5:25-26)

"I feel divine jealousy for you, for I betrothed you to one husband, to present you as a pure virgin to Christ." (2 Corinthians 11:2)

Today, we will examine how the *Kiddushin*, the wedding ceremony, plays in our role as Christ's beloved bride. The word *Kiddushin* means sanctification. It is related to the word *kaddush* (holy). The *kiddushin* is composed of two distinct ceremonies: the *erusin* and *nisuin* or nuptials. We looked into the first part of this wedding ceremony last week, the *erusin*. Once the *erusin* has taken place, the bride has officially entered into her time of betrothal. She is now an official bride/wife. She is a bride because her wedding has begun, and a wife because she has already entered the covenant of marriage with her husband. Hebrew weddings were very different from what we are accustomed to today. When a man and his father came to offer the first cup (the bride price and wedding contract), to a bride and her father, if she accepted, she was considered married from that moment on. It is not like in our current society, where a couple enters a time of engagement while they plan the wedding and can still back out should either party decide to. In Hebrew weddings, once the Kiddushin begins, the couple is already in covenant with one another. To break the covenant would require legal, as well as spiritual recourse.

Let's take a look at a few examples of Kiddushin taking place, look up the following verse and record any thoughts or observations that stand out to you

Genesis 24:45-60

____

____

____

____

____

Genesis 29:13-20

____

____

____

____

____

Matthew 1:18-19

____

____

____

____

As we journey through the steps in a Hebrew wedding, we will see the parallels to our wedding to Christ. However, today we will not so much look into the steps of the wedding as we will examine the concept and meaning of Kiddushin or sanctification.

I find it so endearing that the term used to define the marriage ceremony means sanctification. As one who is married, I can surely see all the ways the Lord uses my own marriage as a great tool to "sanctify" me and make me more like Him. I love that the word symbolizes a process, not a destination. The Greek word for sanctify means; to make holy, consecrate, make clean. Let's reflect on what this actually looks like. Look at the following verse below. In light of what we are learning about how the word for wedding in Hebrew means "sanctify", how might this change your perspective of what the words below mean?

"Husbands, love your wives, as Christ loved the church and gave himself up for her, that he might sanctify her, having cleansed her by the washing of water by the word." (Ephesians 5:25-26)

____

____

____

____

____

Take a moment and personalize the verse above to make it a statement about the process Christ is taking you through in His nuptials to you. Here is my example: *"Rhonda, I love you and gave myself up for you so that I might be able to make you holy, to sanctify (to marry you), and I am going to continue to clean you up and make you more and more beautiful through My Word."*

____

____

____

____

____

It is amazing how one small fact can change our whole perspective on something that we may have felt pretty confident about. So often, our ideas of marriage revolve around the framework of family, children, and even an object for our own happiness and fulfillment. If we truly want to know God and to better understand the truth about Him, as well as the truth about ourselves, and those we love, we must seek to see from His perspective, not our own.

As we consider that God's original title for wedding is based on sanctification, not on family, children, or our own happiness, how might this challenge your perspective on marriage and family?

____

____

____

____

____

I read a book on marriage not long ago that asked this challenging question, "what if marriage is more about making you holy than making you happy?"

We live in a society that idolizes "love" or at least societies' ideas about love. You can't even walk through a supermarket without hearing old love songs while walking past magazines that boast of the rollercoaster ride romances of celebrities. Almost every ounce of media out there today seeks some element of a love story, no matter how perverted or off track. Whether we realize it or not, we are greatly affected by this tidal wave of disinformation. As we seek to understand what love truly is, let's take another look at what God says it is.

Look up the following verses and jot down what they say about love.

1 John 4:16

____

____

____

____

____

1 John 4:19

---

1 Corinthians 13:4-13

Too often we have settled for the world's way off defining love that it is based on feelings, how someone does or does not make us feel. That it is a tool we dispense when one makes us feel good, and we withdraw when one makes us feel bad. However, from God's perspective, He loves us most when we are most difficult, He never based His loves on feelings, but based on His own nature, *"For God is love."* (1 John 4:16) As we consider the relationship that exists between God's marriage to us and His sanctifying of us, we can assume that love often does not make us feel good. It is not fun to know that we need cleansing, much less to go through the process of having to become clean.

If there is one "feeling" we know God experiences towards us based on His word, it is found in the verse below. Please, circle the word that describes God's feeling towards you below.

"I feel divine jealousy for you, for I betrothed you to one husband, to present you as a pure virgin to Christ." (2 Corinthians 11:2)

It is hard to imagine that Christ would experience jealousy for us. It is hard to imagine God as jealous, after all the two just don't seem to go together. However, in Hebrew, the word jealous can also be interpreted to say zealous. One Hebrew scholar describes God's jealousy this way, "For God, His jealously is a measure of His devotion, His passionate caring; for Him it is a fire that consumes His enemies." (hermeneutics.stackexchange.com). I am not God, but I am a momma, and I passionately want what is best for my kids, and I might even be accused of being jealous for who they can become as they walk in surrender to Jesus Christ.

What is God jealous for in the above verse?

____

____

____

____

____

In Himself, He gave us all we need to be cleansed from the stains of the world, to make us pure in the midst of an impure world.

We can't let the world and our own feelings keep us from allowing Him to present us to Christ any longer. There is just no reason to stay impure in our own minds and attitudes; He died so that we can become holy. Now, that is love!

DAY 3

"And the man and his wife were both naked and were not ashamed." (Genesis 2:25)

"Husbands, love your wives, as Christ loved the church and gave himself up for her, that he might sanctify her, having cleansed her by the washing of water with the word." (Ephesians 5:25-26)

In our lesson, we briefly touched on one of the roles of the new Hebrew bride, called Mikvah. Although we will look more fully into how this applies to our lives in week 4, we will spend today taking a glance at how MIKVAH helps us understand our new purpose as Christ's Bride.

Once a woman is betrothed, one of her first acts of submission to this new role is Mikvah. As we discussed in our lesson, Mikvah is Hebrew for baptism (more precisely, immersion). A bride's Mikvah represented her time of ritual cleansing. She would enter a body of living water (a spring or some natural body of pure water), usually with her maidens to attend her. She would enter the body alone, with at least one maiden standing near as witness as she completely submerged herself in the water. She would usually do this at least three times, fluttering her eyelids, and flexing her fingers and toes, to ensure that every single part of her body was touched and purified by the water.

One of the few mentions of the word Mikvah is found in Leviticus 11:36, *"Nevertheless, a spring or a cistern holding water shall be clean, but whoever touches a carcass in them shall be unclean."*

It is listed right in the middle of a long list of instructions about the handling of unclean animals. After reading just a few passages in there, and I am exhausted in trying to remember all the "how to steps" in the process of cleansing from what is unclean. I find it reassuring that when we see Mikvah mentioned here, it is not in association with a "step" or a list of "to dos and don'ts". Mikvah *is* the body of water in which one is cleansed. I find hope here, that amidst all the rules we see placed in religion, and in ourselves, we have a Mikvah, not something "to do" to cleanse ourselves, but a place to enter. We simply must "*be*" in Him, and we are clean.

In fact, one of the other few times we see the word Mikvah mentioned is in Jeremiah 17:12-13. Please, write the verse below and guess which words in the verse translates to Mikvah.

____

____

____

____

I bet as you wrote that verse, you thought it was "*the fountain of living water*" in verse 13. I would have guessed the same, but the word Mikvah is actually found just above that where it says, "*the hope of Israel.*"

The fountain of living water is used to confirm the truth that Jesus, our Mikah is the **hope** of Israel and our hope too. The hope comes with the washing, and oh, what a blessing that we are offered a place of washing.

We see this image again in Zachariah 13:1, "*And on that day there shall be a fountain opened for the house of David and the inhabitants of Jerusalem, to cleanse them from sin and uncleanness.*" If we were to look just a bit further back, we would find another beautiful reference to Jesus. Zachariah 12:10 says, "*And I will pour out on the house of David and the inhabitants of Jerusalem a spirit of grace and pleas for mercy, so that, when they look at me, on him whom they have pierced, they shall mourn for him, as one mourns for an only child, and weep bitterly over him, as one weeps for a firstborn.*"

As I reflect on the above verses, I can't help but try to imagine what it will be like on "that day" for those who will look upon Jesus, and realize that the One they pierced is their Messiah, their fountain of Living Water, the One in Whom they immersed themselves in when they needed cleansing. The only word I can think of to describe how they must feel in that moment is humbled, with a deep sense of wanting to hide themselves from their own truth, yet at the same time great awareness of their need for His greater truth.

What a contrast to the verse we will turn our attention to next. *"And the man and his wife were both naked and were not ashamed." (Genesis 2:25)*

This verse is meticulously placed just after the very first marriage had occurred. God has joined man and woman together and pronounced, *"and they shall become one flesh."* I have often wondered why verse 25 is placed there, mentioned just after the first wedding and just before the fall.

What, in your opinion is God's reason to letting us know that these two were married, and then stood there "naked and not ashamed?"

____

____

____

____

____

Perhaps, it is to point us to a hope that these two can exist together in beauty and harmony. For the life of me, I can't imagine standing anywhere naked and not ashamed. It isn't just my body, but it is something greater. There is vulnerability about being exposed, completely naked in the presence of another. There is fear there; fear of what another thinks and fear of knowing all my imperfections are out there exposed for all to see.

Speaking of being exposed, let's look up the following verses and see if we can grasp an image of what Jesus was "wearing" or not wearing on the Cross. Read the verses below and write down notes about what you find.

John 19:23-24

____

____

____

____

____

Psalm 22:16-18

____

____

____

____

____

Although it is hard for us to imagine that Jesus was crucified naked, there is little doubt left in many Bible scholars' minds that He was. It was customary for Romans to crucify the prisoners with no clothes on. The humiliation and exposure added to the degradation of the punishment. In the case of Jews, we do find that they were often afforded the grace of wearing a loincloth when they were crucified, yet we do not see Jesus being treated with any such dignities at any other part in his arrest, and trial, so we cannot assume that he was offered this one last exemption from his humiliation.

However harsh it is for us to imagine the shame on top of all else that He experienced, in a way it displays a beautiful picture of our beloved Jesus on His wedding day. Just as God pronounced that, _"the two will become one, and "They were both naked and not ashamed,"_ we see our Savior not only becoming our Mikvah during His greatest humiliation, but He also became our husband ,hanging naked and bearing our shame so that He could freely purchase our chance to enter back in to becoming naked and unashamed with Him. Even when we didn't see it, or understand it, He was becoming one with us in every sense of the word. And even though we still can't fully grasp it, He was fulfilling His purpose to make us His bride. When we were most ashamed of Him, He was most **in love** with us.

Love: *Agapao*-indicates a direction of the will and finding one's joy in something. It is used of God's love toward man. It is not based on any merit of the one who receives it, it is complete unselfish love

Here we see love completely making Himself vulnerable to us.

Take a moment to respond to this image below.

____

____

____

____

____

I will never forget the first time this truth came alive in me. I was at a healing retreat, wrestling through childhood trauma that was paralyzing me in every aspect of my life. It was our last day there and I remember being terrified to come back home, and possibly find myself still *stuck* in bonds that I had never, until that point, been able to escape. As we sat around a campfire and listened to the pastor teach, I can't remember exactly what he said, but I knew what God was saying to my heart. As I pondered Him there, naked, powerless and vulnerable on the Cross, knowing that at any moment He could have gotten off, called the whole thing off, and said the same thing to us that I've so often said to Him, *"I don't want to do this anymore."* I could hear His voice bursting though my heart, *"I stayed for you, Rhonda."* And I knew that He *saw, heard, and knew* about all those moments as a child, when I was naked, vulnerable, powerless to get out my situation. The Cross becomes SO big when it becomes so personal.

And there around that fire that morning, I became *unstuck* as I let the reality of all He did for me at the Cross take the weight of all the trauma I had carried in my body since being sexually abused. I made the exchange. And for the first time I could ever remember, I **knew** what it was to be naked and unashamed in His presence.

"Husbands, love your wives, as Christ loved the church and gave himself up for her, that he might sanctify her, having cleansed her by the washing of water with the word." (Ephesians 5:25-26)

"But one of the soldiers pierced his side with a spear, and at once, there came out blood and water." (John 19:34)

"And the Word became flesh and dwelt among us, and we have seen his glory, glory as the only Son from the Father, full of grace and truth." (John 1:14)

Do you see it, beloved? As Jesus' side was pierced, both water and blood came out, *"And on that day there shall be a fountain opened for the house of David and the inhabitants of Jerusalem, to cleanse them from sin and uncleanness."*, Zachariah 13:1. He was fulfilling His role as your beloved husband, *"Husbands, love your wives, as Christ loved the church and gave himself up for her, that he might sanctify her, having cleansed her by the washing of water with the word." (Ephesians 5:25-26)* And He is still doing it today, every time you open His Word, you take a bath, a ritual cleansing, in His unfailing love for you. Just as He, our beloved Word became flesh, so He will never stop cleansing us with His Word until our flesh becomes His Word.

"Therefore a man shall leave his father and his mother and hold fast to his wife, and they shall become one flesh." (Genesis 2:24)

DAY 4

"For you have died, and your life is hidden with Christ in God. When Christ, who is your life appears then you also will appear with him in glory." (Colossians 3:3-4)

"And behold the curtain of the temple was torn in two, from top to bottom. And the earth shook and the rocks were split." (Matthew 37:51)

On day two, we talked about how the word for the wedding ceremony means sanctification. And yesterday, we went a little deeper in understanding how Mikvah (the ceremonial cleaning of the bride) plays a role in this sanctification. Today, we will talk about the title the bride is given once she enters this marriage covenant as we seek to understand more about how we, as Christ's bride, must live out our identity in Him. The name given for a Hebrew bride once she has entered the marriage nuptials is *Kal'lah*. It means secluded one or enclosed one. The name originates from the ceremony where the bride is veiled once she has accepted and entered the marriage covenant with her betrothed. One of the last steps in the first part of the marriage covenant takes place just before the groom leaves with his father to go back to his father's house and prepare a place for his bride to live with him (the bridal chamber). He says, *"I go to prepare a place for you."* And as he does, he veils his bride, which offers a sign to the outside world that this woman is taken, that she now belongs to her husband. It also represents that her time of separation from her old life has now begun. That, even though she will physically remain in her old home, she is now "set apart" for her new home with her beloved. Before this happened, she was under the care and authority of her father, but now all that has transferred to her husband. She is now a *Kal'lah,* a bride. And so are you, beloved.

As we consider how this "setting apart" takes place, take a moment below and write out your thoughts about how this ritual relates to your own life in Christ.

____

____

____

____

____

There are so many implications about what "the veiling" means to us as Christ's bride and I encourage you to search out and study on your own every ounce of scripture pertaining to them all. Today, we will consider just a few ways in which we see this ritual being paralleled in scripture.

Let's first meet in Hebrews 9 and read verses 1-10 together. Then answer the questions below.

In verse 3 what is the place that stands behind the second curtain called?

____

____

____

____

____

Verse 7 speaks about whom and under what conditions one can enter the place behind the second curtain. Who can enter and under what conditions is he able to enter?

____

____

____

____

____

Let's skip down to Hebrews 9:24-28. Answer the questions below after reading these verses.

What does it say in verse 24 about "the holy places made with hands?"

____

____

____

____

____

Verse 26 talks about how Christ put away all sin, what does this verse say about that?

____

____

____

____

____

I love how verse 24 uses the words, *"which are copies of the true things."* There is an idea alluded to here that what we know and see in this world, which seems so real to us, is not necessarily a *true thing.* But you, beloved, the moment you decided to become the bride of Christ, you became a *true thing.* You became one with the One Whom all things on earth only exist to point to. He is the real thing, and we become real only when we become His *Ka'lah,* His enclosed one. He tears the veil that has separated us from Him and encloses us in Himself.

The verse below gives us a beautiful example of what it means to be Christ's *Ka'lah.* Please, personalize this verse below by adding your name in the blank spaces.

"For you have died, and your life is hidden with Christ in God. When Christ, who is your life appears then you also will appear with him in glory." (Colossians 3:3-4)

"For, _______________ has died, and _______________'s life is hidden with Christ in God. When Christ, who is _______________'s life appears then _______________ will appear with Him in glory.

There is another aspect of the veiling that we need to consider. Let's begin by examining our own definitions of the word veil.

Take a moment and write your own definition of the word veil below.

____

____

____

____

____

Now, let's meet in 2 Corinthians 3:14-18. After reading the verses, answer the questions below.

In verses 14 - 16, there are comments made about a veil and how that veil is taken away. What does it say about where the veil exists and how it is taken away?

____

____

____

____

____

In verses 17-18, we see an amazing confirmation about what happens to us once the veil is removed. What does it say we are able to behold with unveiled faces?

____

____

____

____

There is one word that is mentioned 3 times in those two verses, what is that word?

____

____

____

____

____

In your own words, describe what the Spirit and the lifting of the veil have in common with one another.

____

____

____

____

____

Verse 17 seems to stand out like a sore thumb. Right there in the middle of the passage about how the veil stays over the hearts of those who still seek the law, yet is lifted when one turns to Christ we see these words, *"Now the Lord is Spirit, and where the Spirit of the Lord is, there is freedom."* At first glance, it seems to not belong. However, as we look deeper into the concept of the veil and what this has to do with freedom, we can see something wonderful.

In Greek the definition for the word veil is, *to wrap around, as bark, shell, or plaster, to cover up.*

At first glance we may not completely be able to *"wrap"* our minds around how the Spirit has everything to do with our freedom. Once we are in Christ, the veil is removed, even though the outside world looks completely the same with our physical eyes. It looks completely different with our hearts because we have been "enclosed" with Christ; therefore, we are able to see everything from His perspective, with His eyes. God is Spirit, and once His Spirit is alive in us, we have a completely new way of seeing, no longer through a veil, but through the very eyes of Christ, our Bridegroom. In earthly marriage, even though we make commitments and express vows that we will become one with one another, we are not truly able to because our sin and selfishness keep us separate in so many ways. However, in our marriage to Christ, we **truly do become one with Him**. Once He "encloses" us within Himself, even though we don't always access our new sight available to us through His Spirit, He never stops accessing His new sight towards us. We walk by faith, not by sight. He sees us through the reality of His sacrifice for us at the Cross, even when we don't see ourselves in that light. He never forgets or takes for granted that He is married to us, even though we so often forget.

Let's close by looking into this concept in 2 Corinthians 4:3-6. In your own words below, describe the difference between how the world sees and how we, the bride of Christ, see.

____

____

____

____

____

Now that the veil from our face is finally removed, let's look around some more. Meet me in John 19:28-30. The words, "it is finished" represent one word, *tetelesti*, in Aramaic. It is truly a beautiful word, a word that an artist would use when he had finished his last paint stroke, seeing that nothing more could be added to perfect his work or perhaps the word that a builder would use as he hands over the keys to a newly built home, no stone is left unturned. Nothing more can be added to complete this piece of work.

Just imagine it, beloved, before you were ever born, the dream of you existed in Christ's heart and there was a moment when He looked up to the Father and pronounced to Him about you, *"Tetelesti!* She is finished, there is nothing more needed to perfect her!"* And with that, He gave Himself permission to stop breathing, to stop wearing the sins of the world. For your Mohar (bride price), had been paid in full with the precious blood of Jesus.

Let's look at what happened just after this, *"And behold the curtain of the temple was torn in two, from top to bottom. And the earth shook and the rocks were split." (Matthew 37:51)* The temple's curtain represented the separation of God and man. It hung in between the Holy Place in the temple separating it from the Most Holy Place, the place where the ark of the covenant was placed. The Most Holy Place was where God would meet with the High Priest, as he made atonement for the sins of God's people. When Christ died, this curtain ripped from top to bottom, God Himself, finally beholding His bride fully, without sin for the first time since the Fall.

DAY 5

"And while they were going to buy, the bride-groom came, and those who were ready went in with him to the marriage feast, and the door was shut." (Matthew 25:10)

"In Him was life, and that life was the light of men. The light shines in the darkness and the darkness has not overcome it." (John 1:4-5)

The last ritual we will consider this week from the Hebrew wedding has to do with the bride's heart of expectancy towards her new husband. After he left, she would place an oil lamp in her window and each night as the darkness fell, she would light the lamp. This action symbolized to her beloved that she was waiting for him, that she was holding on to his promise to come back for her. His last words to her before he left were, *"I go to prepare a place for you."* At that, he and his father would leave and go back home. Shortly after, the bridegroom would begin to build a bridal chamber for his *Ka'lah.* The process of building this chamber was very tedious and labor intensive. You see, this bridegroom was not only building this chamber for his bride, but it also had to be built according to his father's specifications and, before this groom could go get his bride, he must have his father's word of approval. Each day, the groom would work on the bridal chamber, perfecting it as he listened to his father's instructions about what more was needed in order to complete this home for, he and his bride. He, nor his bride to be, would ever know when the fulfillment of the wedding would take place. Only the father knew, and only at his word was the "go get your bride," given. At times when the groom would need an encouragement or reminder as to why he was doing all of this work, he could look into his bride's window and see the lamp burning and know that she was waiting for him, her love and expectancy were keeping her heart awake with the anticipation of his coming. As the chamber neared completion, the groom worked even more diligently, knowing that his time apart from his bride was nearing completion. Soon, his father would give the word and he and his groomsmen would begin the journey of wedding celebration as he went to get his bride and take her to the place, the bridal chamber he had been preparing for her. The long-awaited word from the father often came at night, and the celebration would begin as music, torches, and lamps would light up the atmosphere all around them and people would come out of their homes to join the wedding celebration.

Let's look at some scripture references to this portion of the wedding. Look up the following verses and record how they relate to this portion of the wedding.

John 14:1-3

____

____

____

____

____

Matthew 24:36 & 44

____

____

____

____

____

Matthew 25

____

____

____

____

____

The above scriptures reference the need for the bride to be prepared for the completion of her wedding, the moment when she will see her groom face to face. However, there is a need for us to look further into what our part is in keeping that lamp lit. For it is His job, our groom Jesus, to build the home for us. But it is our job to keep our lamps well-trimmed and lit, placed in the window of our heart, so that at any time, our Beloved can look at us and be encouraged and reminded that we are expecting Him, that we have not forgotten the promises He made to us when He married us.

The first question that comes to mind when I consider what keeping our lamp lit is, how? Well, let's look at the scriptures below and record what they have to say about the relationship that exists between lamps, light, and oil.

Psalm 119:105

____

____

____

____

____

John 1:4-9

____

____

____

____

____

John 8:12

____

____

____

____

____

1 John 1:5-7

____

____

____

____

____

Luke 12:35-37

____

____

____

____

____

Revelation 21:23-24

____

____

____

____

____

There is so much here to understand about what our relationship is to the Light. As Christ's bride, He is our Light. In so many ways, He has already come for us; His Spirit is already alive in us. However, we are to stay alert and awake, waiting for that moment when what we already know and live in His spirit becomes our reality; that day when our faith becomes our sight. Jesus already came for us, He already married us, but there is a whole other aspect of our marriage relationship that we have not experienced yet. In His Kingdom, the abstract comes before the concrete. We must understand the spiritual before we can lay hold of the physical. Once we became His, we became spiritual beings, and we must relate to Him in spirit and in truth. Part of our role as His bride here on earth is to maintain the connection to Him through His Word. John 1 reminds us that, *"the Word became flesh."* Long before you ever acknowledged Him, He came for you. He became flesh so that He could not only be qualified to die for our sins, but also so He could have compassion for us, so that He could know what it is like to live in this atmosphere, in the weakness of human flesh. One of the greatest ways we can honor our marriage to Him is in honoring Him through laying hold of what it means to live in His atmosphere, to display our faith in Him and in His Word and to know that we not only belong to Him, but to live like we know we belong to Him. We allow Him to conform us into His image, and likeness.

In what ways right now do you feel you are honoring your marriage to Christ in living like you belong to Him?

____

____

____

____

____

In what ways do you sense Him challenging you to allow His light to become brighter in you?

____

____

____

____

____

One thing that helped me comprehend this more readily was when I went back to the beginning to look at when God first created light.

Let's meet in Genesis 1:1-5, read the verses and answer the questions that follow.

In verse 2, how is the earth described?

____

____

____

____

Verse 3 mentions God's first creation, what is it?

____

____

____

____

In verse 4 what does it say God separated?

____

____

____

____

According to these verses, what existed first, darkness or light?

____

____

____

____

Our concept of time is a little different than that of the Hebrews. We consider a new day when the sun comes up. It is opposite for them. A new day comes when the sun goes down and is extended when the sun comes up in the morning.

In our understanding of time, the darkness comes and overtakes the light. Our days end in darkness. For them, the Light comes and overtakes the darkness. Their day ends in light.

Beloved, when you became His, the Light came and overtook your darkness. Each time you open your bible, pray and share your heart with Christ, you exercise faith in choosing to believe that what He says about you is true instead of what you or others say, you are letting more and more of His Light overshadow your darkness.

"In Him was life, and that life was the light of men. The light shines in the darkness and the darkness has not overcome it." (John 1:4-5)

"You are all children of the light and children of the day. We do not belong to the night or to darkness." (1 Thessalonians 5:5)

These words take on new life when we view them in context of our lives, our hearts, and not just in context of the world that we live in.

Let's close our study today by affirming this truth. And in doing so, allow our Beloved to see that we are placing the lamp of our faith in Him in the window of our heart. May He see it and be blessed in knowing that His bride is awaiting and looking forward to His coming for her.

Here is my personalization: *In Him was life, and that life was the light of Rhonda. The light shines in Rhonda's darkness and Rhonda's darkness has not overcome it.*

Rhonda is a child of the light and of the day, she does not belong to the night or darkness.

____

____

____

____

____

Look, I see the Son rising in you already! You are a radiant bride!

Week 3:
You+Jesus=One

DAY   1

"So they are no longer two but one flesh. What therefore God has joined together, let not man separate." (Matthew 19:6)

"And God said, "Let there be light," and there was light." (Genesis 1:3)

Rejection, it is the one word that encapsulates my greatest fears on earth. Even now as I walk with Christ into new places of ever-expanding revelation of His love, I find the fear of rejection still arises within me. Although He and I have come so far, He never stops moving me forward and showing me the truth about myself. So often, the root of this fear springs up in new ways, in new places in my heart, and even as I conquer new territory, this is the one area in my walk with Christ that I tend to wrestle with most often. I have often heard it said that we spend most of our adult lives overcoming our childhood. The longer I walk with Christ, the more I tend to believe this; that we enter this world completely dependent on man, we grow up with the goal of completely relying on self, and never really rest until we grow completely dependent on God, our Father. So often the scars we experience as children leave marks on our lives that serve as our springboards later as we grow up, helping us dive in to understanding our soul's greatest need, our need for God. Like Adam's missing rib, we know something inside us is gone and we search for a filling to make us whole again. Although these scars leave reminders of great pain, they also point to our greatest invitations to our need for

Christ. In ways we don't always understand, our scars here on earth represent one-way Jesus beckons us to Himself, and once our scars are paired with the Holy Spirit, perhaps we awaken to a desire to exchange our scars for His. *"...Put your finger here, and see my hands, and put out your hand, and place it in my side. Do not disbelieve, but believe."* (John 20:28b)

My greatest scar has been rejection. My earliest memories consist of great fear. As the middle child of parents who divorced when I was very young, I can't remember a time when I did not long to be loved, embraced, and cherished. Unfortunately, because the circumstances of my life opened the door for darkness to enter in, the enemy found a way for me to be loved, adored, and cherished in profane ways. Before I could even read, the enemy was already scripting the story of my life, and it was a story of rejection and destruction.

What about you? If you could give a name to your greatest scar, what would it be? And why?

____

____

____

____

____

It is both beautiful and perplexing how Christ uses the very scars in our lives to draw us to Him. There is a mystery and tension that exists in our knowing that Jesus is not the author of our scars, yet He does allow them. This tension kept me from Him so long as I tried to wrestle my past off me, trusting in my own false light for years. Yet, the tension never left until, worn out and exasperated, I finally gave in to the small, yet strong voice in my heart saying, *"why don't you try surrendering instead of understanding, Rhonda."* That was the beginning of my exchange, that was my wedding day.

In our homework last week, we examined how the Israelites do not view time in the same way that we do, for them, a new day begins at dusk, and the morning sunrise gives testimony to the light overcoming the darkness. Just as in the beginning God commanded light to shine out of darkness, so His ways are still evident in His coming for our hearts. Let's spend some time going back to the start and seeing how these verses apply to our lives.

Meet me in Genesis 1:1-4. Read the verses and answer the questions below.

What was in the beginning, light or darkness, water or dry land?

____

____

____

____

____

What did God call good? And in verse 4, what did He do as soon as He said that it was good?

____

____

____

____

____

In my opinion, one of the greatest hindrances to the world seeing Jesus in us is that we mistakenly believe that it is *our* light that keeps us in God's Presence. There is even a song that we learn in church as children that promotes this idea. It goes, *"this little light of mine, I'm gonna let it shine..."* There is nothing little about God's light and there is surely no light in us that we can shine. In fact, we do not even have the ability to let any light shine. John 1 testifies that He is the light that shines out of the darkness. Therefore, just as the Israelites believe that the darkness comes first, and then the light comes to overtake the darkness, so it is with us. We give Him our darkness and He gives us His light. And once this exchange takes place, His light can't help but shine in us, whether we *let* it or not.

What are the areas of darkness in your life right now? Darkness can represent areas of sin, unbelief, unhealed pain, or simply areas where we are unable to "see" what is in front of us. If you aren't sure, take a moment to pray and ask Jesus. Take time to let Him show you.

____

____

____

____

____

Beloved, as you acknowledge these areas before the Lord, He hovers over them and calls His light to shine upon them. As soon as you release them into His hands, He shines His truth on it and calls it good, it may not feel good when we are experiencing it here on earth, yet there is beauty in watching light overtake darkness, and there is beauty in allowing His light to come and rise on our hearts. And just as He did in the very beginning, so He still does. He begins to separate the darkness from the light. What once was so unclear to us, He brings the light of the glory of His face into and even though we may not see our circumstances change overnight, we get to see His light shining out of our darkness-and that, beloved, is good!

Let's take a moment here and write a prayer confessing our faith that His Light will overcome our darkness.

____

____

____

____

____

"So they are no longer two but one flesh. What therefore God has joined together, let no man separate." (Matthew 19:6)

The words above were spoken by Jesus when Pharisees tested Him by asking Him about divorce. I love how Jesus does not go into some argument about when and why divorce is lawful. He simply answers their question with the truth of His Father's words. In other words, they wanted to ask about what was in the dark, and instead of addressing the darkness, Jesus appeals to the Light.

Beloved, He does the same with us. Even now, there are so many questions that I have regarding areas of my life that there seems to be a darkness over, areas where I just can't see what is right ahead of me. As I open the doors to my heart to Him and express my concerns, I can hear Him assuring me that, *"even the darkness is not dark to Me, the night is bright as the day, for darkness is as light with Me," (based on Psalm 139:12).* Once I have given it to Him, it is no longer dark. Once my darkness is wed to His light, His light will overcome my darkness as sure as a sunrise will overcome the night. And once His light comes, we can no more separate ourselves from Him than we can separate the light of the sun from the dark of the night.

We can never extinguish His light, but we can reject it. Remember that love does not exist without choice. Just as we discussed earlier, we can hinder His light from coming by attempting to shine our own. We can forget that it was our darkness He came for, not our light (for we have none of our own to give).

What does 2 Corinthians 11:14 say about false light?

____

____

____

____

____

Let's take a moment here to ask the Lord to reveal to us if there is any area in our lives where we are hindering His light from coming because we are trying to shine our own. Initial here once you have prayed_________

____

____

____

____

Please, use the space below to write about what God is showing you regarding His light verses your own.

____

____

____

____

____

Beloved, what God has joined together, let no flesh (including your own) separate. Let's close in prayer thanking God for allowing His light to shine into our darkness.

DAY 2

"...when Israel sought for rest, the LORD appeared to him from far away. I have loved you with an everlasting love; therefore I have continued my faithfulness to you." (Jeremiah 31:2)

"Although he was a son, he learned obedience through what he suffered. And being made perfect, he became the source of eternal salvation to all who obey him." (Hebrews 5:8-9)

I mentioned yesterday that my greatest childhood scar is rejection. We also talked about how Christ's light shines into our darkness and overcome it. This is part of His fulfillment of His ketubah to us (His wedding contract). Today, we will look deeper into how Christ uses the most unlikely source to draw us towards Him, our pain.

Let's start in Hebrews 5:7-9. Read the verses and then answer the questions below.

In verse 7 how is Jesus' demeanor described as He prayed? And to whom was He praying?

____

____

____

____

____

In verse 8, how does it say that Jesus learned obedience?

____

____

____

____

____

In verse 9 how does it describe the relationship that exist between eternal salvation and obedience?

____

____

____

____

____

We mistakenly often take for granted not only Christ's death on the Cross for our sins, but also His life of obedience in the flesh which made Him qualified to take our flesh to the Cross. It is not easy for us to live in obedience and was not easy for Him as well.

As we consider the role of the matchmaker in the Hebrew wedding, we must first consider how suffering plays such a large part in drawing us to our beloved Jesus.

Although I know many who received Christ at a young age and have walked with Him since then, I do not know many who grew in knowledge of Him without going through times of suffering. In our broken world, suffering is inescapable and unavoidable. Regardless of what we might imagine others' lives to be like, there are none who do not walk through the effects of sin. There are none who can come through this world without experiencing the pain associated with it. In Christ we have great hope, but it is not because our circumstances magically change once we receive Him, or at least not always right away. We change, and as we respond to His life in us, our world around us can't help but reflect the new hope that belongs to us. We have great hope, because in Him, we are enabled to live above this world and free from it.

Let's look at what I mean by this, meet me in John 17, let's read it together.

Write any thoughts that stand out to you below.

____

____

____

____

____

Out of all the chapters in the Bible, this is one of my favorites. Not only is it a prayer that we can read and take in with our eyes, but also perfectly portrays His heart towards us. He desires that we be One with Him, that we belong not to this world, but to Him. He affirms that we are not part of this world, even though we are still in it. One of the most perplexing and beautiful parts of this prayer that affirms how suffering leads us to Christ is found in verse 1 where Jesus prays, *"Father, the hour has come; glorify your Son that your Son may glorify you."* This was just before He was going to the Cross, the moment His greatest suffering wed His greatest glory. We see here that there is a relationship between suffering and glory.

In your own words, describe what relationship you see between suffering and glory.

____

____

____

____

____

Do you know anyone who has personified this relationship? Please, describe.

____

____

____

____

I have watched two dear friends lose babies. There is nothing I fear more on earth than this kind of loss. Yet as these mommas stood during what would be my worst nightmare, I watched the ground beneath their feet become sacred, and holy. There was absolutely no doubt Who was holding them up, sustaining them, and giving their empty arms a filling that only the glory of heaven could sustain. There is something beautiful, holy and I dare say even supernatural about seeing a mom whose arms had to just let go of what she thought she never could, raised in worship as she entrusts her little one into the arms of the One Who she knows is holding her and her baby together in a place that is above this world. I never forget moments like those, for I **see** heaven touch earth in them, through fragile and broken human hearts, I see Jesus.

Let's take another look at some scriptures that may help us understand how God can often use suffering to become our matchmaker. Look up the following verses and record what they say about suffering.

____

____

____

____

____

Romans 5:3-5

____

____

____

____

Romans 8:18

____

____

____

____

Hebrews 2:9-10

____

____

____

____

1 Peter 5:6-10

____

____

____

____

____

In our society today there is little observance of how suffering plays out in relationship. Whether we realize it or not, we have all bought into the idea that we prefer to stay away from those people or circumstances which bring us pain. Yet, we see here that our greatest relationship we could ever be a part of came through greatest suffering. I don't know how you came to know Christ, but for me, it happened when my greatest fear came head-to-head with my greatest pain. It happened when all hope of ever escaping rejection came to an end, and I had to face the truth about myself that I was never going to find the perfect someone who would not reject me, that my hope of finding security in this life did not exist in someone with skin on. I came to the realization that the problem with me did not lie in how others treated me; the problem with me **was me!** It took so much suffering to get me to this point, and in my moment of greatest pain and hopelessness, I took the one hope that was held out to me in the form of Jesus' hand. I no longer was going to try and fill the void in my heart with what I felt was lacking, I was going to exchange my heart for His, and leave the filling of all voids to His hands.

What about you, what brought you to Christ? Or is bringing you to Him?

____

____

____

____

____

"...when Israel sought for rest, the LORD appeared to him from far away. I have loved you with an everlasting love; therefore I have continued my faithfulness to you." (Jeremiah 31:2)

Beloved, before you were ever born, your Husband was pursuing you. Before you even had circumstances that you would need rest from, He had already provided it. From far away Jesus appeared and began pursuing you with His love. Before you ever knew what suffering was, He not only provided a way for you to reach beyond your suffering, He also provided a way to reach into your suffering and experience His love for you right in the middle of it. He has already reached into every moment of your darkness, and is waiting with the lamp of His light to walk you right through it. You are **never** alone

How does your perspective of your current and future moments of darkness change as you consider that His light is already waiting for you in every single moment of darkness you will ever face? Please, share below.

____

____

____

____

____

Let's close with a prayer thanking Him for His unfailing, never-ending light!

DAY 3

"And I will ask the Father, and he will give you another Helper, to be with you forever, even the Spirit of truth, whom the world cannot receive, because it sees him nor knows him. You know him for he dwells with you and will be in you." (John 14:16-17)

"And the rib that the LORD God had taken out from the man he made into a woman and brought her to the man." (Genesis 2:22)

The Hebrew custom of *Shidduch* (matchmaking) is still embraced today, in fact there are matchmaking websites dedicated to this custom of helping Hebrew couples find their perfect match, the one whom God has foreordained them to be with. The *Shidduch* is a system of matchmaking in which the Jewish singles are introduced to one another in orthodox Jewish communities for the purpose of marriage. Orthodox Jewish families see matchmaking as a mitzvah (commandment from God). The *Shidduch* provides opportunities for families from both sides to enquire about such things as; character, intelligence, level of learning, financial status, family and health status, appearance, and level of religious observance of potential mates. The *Shidduch* stems from a Hebrew belief in *Bashert*, which is Hebrew for destiny. It is the idea that whom one marries has been foreordained by God, and God created the one who will perfectly complement the other. This belief even goes so far as to subscribe to the idea that when God creates a man before he is born, He takes the woman whom he will one day marry out of his side and set her apart for him to one day find and marry under His own supervision and providence.

It is truly a beautiful idea and one that we will look closely at today as we see how this plays out in our own marriage with Christ, with the Holy Spirit as our *Shidduch,* our Matchmaker.

Before we look further in to how this applies in our own lives, let's look at where this idea originally came from. Let's examine the very first wedding and see if we can grasp some new insight.

Meet me in Genesis 2 and let's read verses 18-25 together and then answer the questions below.

In verse 18, who first noticed that Adam was alone? Is there any mention from Adam of needing a wife?

____

____

____

____

____

In verses 19 and 20, how does God first respond to seeing that it was not good for Adam to be alone?

____

____

____

____

____

In your opinion, why would God make Adam name the animals as a first response to what He already knew that Adam needed?

____

____

____

____

____

What do you think God might be trying to help Adam perceive through naming the animals?

____

____

____

____

What might this have to do with God's plans to provide him a helper suitable for him?

____

____

____

____

How might this apply in your life right now? Is there a need that you know God must know about, but it seems like He is making you "name each animal" before He gets around to providing what you need?

____

____

____

____

If so, what do you think He might be wishing you to perceive?

____

____

____

____

____

Imagine Adam sitting there as the animals came, two by two, to be named by him. And as he is naming them, he is noticing something, "male, female…there are two of them, but only one of me." Perhaps he expressed this observation to God, we don't know for sure because the Word does not say, but we do know that God knew his need and that before Adam even had the desire for a wife, God had already planned to fulfill it.

These passages affirm the words of Jesus in Matthew 6:8, *"…For your Father knows what you need before you ask Him."*

Let's get back to our reading in Genesis, now look at verses 21-22, and answer the following questions

In verse 21, what was Adam doing while God was creating his helper?

____

____

____

____

____

What did God use to form the woman? And where did He get this?

____

____

____

____

____

In verse 22, who brought the woman to Adam? What does this say about who is to bring us to our mate?

____

____

____

____

____

We can assume based on what we have just seen, that long before there was a word for it, God was in the business of matchmaking. Just as He was in the beginning, so He is with us in our "matchmaking" to Christ. We see evidence of this in Christ own words in John 14:16-17, *"And I will ask the Father, and he will give you another Helper, to be with you forever, even the Spirit of truth, whom the world cannot receive, because it sees him nor knows him. You know him for he dwells with you and will be in you."* The Holy Spirit plays many roles in our marriage to Christ, the first of which is *Shidduch*.

Now, let's get back to the first wedding and examine how this wedding parallels our own. In verse 23 we see Adam's first response to seeing God's gift to him, please write the words he says about her below.

____

____

____

____

In ancient times the authority to name implied authority to govern. Adam named his wife, not out of celebration of his authority over her, but out of celebration in who she was and the gift of God in making her. I can almost picture this moment, with tears of joy in his eyes and so much appreciation for who she is he impulsively proclaims the very first poem, "At last, there is someone for me and she is made from me" And then, instinctively we see God celebrating this moment with perhaps, His most beautiful creation of all – marriage.

In verses 24, what does God say about the process of marriage?

____

____

____

____

____

And my favorite is verse 25, *"And the man and his wife were both naked and were not ashamed."* I cannot even imagine a wedding in which the bride and groom are nude.

It seems perverted today but that is because sin has tried to pervert all of God's creations, especially marriage and sexuality. But in the beginning, when God made marriage, there was no perversion in it for there was no shame. The very first marriage was based on complete intimacy, and transparency with God, man and woman. It was pure and beautiful. As we will see this week, our marriage to Jesus portrays so many of the same elements.

Let's take a moment and investigate the idea of *Bashert* (Hebrew for destiny).

Let's look back at Genesis 1:26-31. After reading these verses, please, answer the questions below.

Who is God creating in these verses?

____

____

____

____

____

In verse 27 whose image does it say that they are made in?

____

____

____

____

____

In verse 26 who does He give dominion to?

____

____

____

____

____

We see in these verses the account of God creating man and woman, yet in Chapter 2 we see a different account of how this all came about. Chapter 1 gives us the creation account, while Chapter 2 gets more specific about God's creation of man and woman, the crown of His creation. There is order given, as well as responsibility given.

According to Genesis 2:15-17, who was given the responsibility to maintain life through obeying God?

____

____

____

____

____

We know that it was Adam; for these instructions were given before Eve was even created. This is important to know when we consider Christ's *Ketubah* for us (His wedding contract). As we look at these two chapters, we can see that our matchmaker is God Himself, and we can also see the idea of *Bashert* taking place as we see woman literally taken out of man, formed from him, and for him.

Let's close with a prayer thanking Him for being our *Shidduch* as well as our *Bashert*.

DAY 4

"Then the man said, 'This at last is bone of my bones and flesh of my flesh; so she shall be called Woman, because she was taken out of Man.'" (Genesis 2:23)

"But one of the soldiers pierced his side with a spear, and at once there came out blood and water." (John 19:24)

"And this is he who came by water and blood —Jesus Christ; not by water only but by the water and the blood. And the Spirit is the one who testifies, because the Spirit is the truth. For there are three that testify; the Spirit and the water and the blood; and these three agree." (1 John 5:6-8)

Yesterday, we looked briefly into the idea that Christ is our Bashert, our destiny. Today we will explore this concept more. One scholar quoted a highly respected rabbi *Rav Judah* as saying, *"Forty days before the formation of a child, a heavenly voice issues forth and proclaims, 'The daughter of this person is for that person; the house of this person is for that person; the field of this person is for that person!'"* The idea that God is the only One who truly knows who we are destined to marry is a deeply cherished belief that is still prevalent the Jewish faith today. This idea is also manifested in our Biblical doctrine of predestination.

Look up the following verses and record what they say about Christ being our Bashert; our destiny,

Romans 8:29-30

____

____

____

____

____

Ephesians 1:3-6

____

____

____

____

____

To be honest, the idea of being predestined often confused me and led me to such questions as, "if Christ already knows who He has chosen, why does He ask us to go and tell the world the good news?" To me it seems pointless, but as I learn more about the Hebrew wedding and about the idea of Bashert, I am greatly encouraged and learning to see so much about the Bible that supports His marriage to us. For, when we look at this idea through the eyes of a bride, I see great romance in it all. Just as we love a good love story, so does our Bridegroom. In a way, Bashart (or predestination) ensures that we each get our own individual love story with our Savior and Groom. There is beauty, mystery, and near misses as the two lovers finally unite and become one with the One they were always meant for.

To better understand the role Bashart plays in our union with Christ, we must also look at the Cross.

On day 1-3 of this week, we spent a lot of time in Genesis 1-3. Before we go further into our lesson for today, let's review some concepts that will come in to play with what we are learning today. Please, answer the following questions based on what we learned earlier this week.

Who created woman?

____

____

____

____

____

Where did she come from?

____

____

____

____

____

What was Adam doing while she was made?

____

____

____

____

Now, let's jump over to John 19:33-34. Read the verses and answer the following questions.

What state was Christ in when this happened?

____

____

____

____

What came out of His side?

____

____

____

____

"But one of the soldiers pierced his side with a spear, and at once there came out blood and water." (John 19:24)

Now, let's look at 1 John 5:6-8, *"And this is he who came by water and blood - Jesus Christ; not by water only but by the water and the blood. And the Spirit is the one who testifies, because the Spirit is the truth. For there are three that testify; the Spirit and the water and the blood; and these three agree."*

Beloved, this may be difficult to conceive but just as Eve was taken out the side of Adam while he was sleeping, so you and I were taken out of the side of Jesus Christ, while He was sleeping (dead on the Cross). Just as God took a rib from Adam's side to fashion woman, so He opened a place for us through Christ's side to fashion us. As the blood and water poured from the side of Christ, spilling out from His broken heart, so we were fashioned at the foot of the Cross, formed from the water and blood that poured out of the heart of Jesus. The rib is a bone that protects the vital organs in a body, the heart and the lungs. A wife was originally created to be a helper and protector of mans' heartbeat and breath. She was meant to be the one person in the world whom he could make himself vulnerable to, whom he could expose his areas of greatest weakness to. Beloved, Christ came and exposed Himself fully to us, literally until He gave up all there was, until it was finished, and all His strength was poured out of Him and left here for us, His Bride. Just like in the garden so long ago when the first wife was formed, there was a moment when Jesus breathed His last, the blood and water from His side was spilled, mixing with the dirt at the foot of the Cross, creating a whole new being, the bride of Christ!

In that moment of greatest humiliation, there was great glory, for at last Jesus could look at you and me and say, *"This at last is bone of my bones and flesh of my flesh; so she shall be called Woman, because she was taken out of Man." (Genesis 2:23.)*

Please, take a moment and record a prayer of gratitude below for your beloved Bridegroom, Jesus, coming to make you His own.

____

____

____

____

____

We will close with a look at what our future is to soon become. Let's meet in Revelation 21:9-27.

Who are these verses written about?

____

____

____

____

____

In these verses, the bride is portrayed as a great city, a very beautiful city. In verses 22-23, Who is the Temple?

____

____

____

____

____

How is the city lit?

____

____

____

____

____

Beloved, we are the city on a hill, and He is our Lamp and our Light, and God is our Temple, *"and they shall become one flesh."* (Gen, 2:24b). Each part of us is a greater whole, yet each distinct in purpose. We are one yet working together in perfect harmony. This is our marriage beloved, the way it was created to be from the beginning; God, the Bridegroom and His bride. We are one with Him now, and we shall be one with Him always.

DAY 5

"...your desire shall be for your husband, and he shall rule over you." (Genesis 3:16b)

"Then turning to the disciples he said privately, "Blessed are the eyes that see what you see! For I tell you that many prophets and kings desired to see what you see, and did not see it, and hear what you hear, and did not hear it." (Luke 10:23-24)

The longer I walk with Jesus, the more I grow to understand that I must be careful in making any assumptions about Him. His kingdom is completely and utterly different from this world, in fact, it seems to be almost an upside-down kingdom in terms of what we perceive a kingdom to be.

In His kingdom, the way up is down, and vice versa. In His kingdom, the more one let's go of on earth, the more he may lay claim to in heaven. This is a kingdom where some of our greatest treasures were prepared for us in prisons, while some of the greatest horrors took place in palaces. It is an inside-out kingdom where what matters most in a man is the content of his heart, not the contents of his home. In this kingdom we gain most by what we can see in faith, and we must let go of what we see with our eyes. It is a kingdom that does not consist of rules and regulations, but of love and relationship. And it with this thought, beloved, that we will examine our first scripture for today's lesson.

Let's meet again in Genesis 3 and let's read about how God responds to the woman after she had eaten from the tree of knowledge of good and evil.

Look at verses 14 - 16 and answer the following questions based on what God says.

In verse 14 -15, He is talking to the serpent, what does He say the serpent will eat all the days of his life?

____

____

____

____

____

What is man made from (hint, it is mentioned in vs. 19)?

____

____

____

____

____

Dust, it may seem like a small detail, but we will find that nothing in God's Word is small, and everything has great significance. When we see this spoken of in God's Word, we catch a glimpse of the futility that man is now subject to due to sin entering the world. His whole life he will work the ground from which he was taken until he returns to it. Not only that, but the serpent will be eating, consuming dust all the days of his life. We can overlook this and miss the great glimpse we are given here of the relationship that man and the serpent now are entering in to. All the days of human life, he will not only have to work the ground, but he will also have the frustration of the serpent now striving to consume him as he fulfills his earthly existence. There is a hopelessness to it all, that is until we look at what God has spoken of about woman.

Let's take another look at verse 15, what two areas that can bring us hope are mentioned here?

____

____

____

____

Until this point, Adam and Eve have not had any children. And God mentions here that not only will they have "*offspring*", but also that hope will come through that offspring. Speaking to the serpent He says, *"he shall bruise your head, and you shall bruise his heel." (Gen. 3:15b).* A bruise to the heel is painful for us. As we walk out our time on earthly sod, our feet are subject to the ground, which is now cursed, and we are now exposed and vulnerable to the serpent who is eating dust all the days of his life. Being human is hard, and it hurts. Just living is difficult; every single one of us walks with bruised heels on a painful path here on earth, yet those of us who know Christ walk with great hope. For, as we look at God's words to the serpent again, we can see that his head is bruised. We receive a painful blow, but he receives a fatal one. A bruise to the head is a mortal wound.

We see the word bruise again mentioned in Isaiah 53:10. The King James version states the verse like this, "*Yet it pleased the LORD to bruise him; he hath put him to grief; when though shalt make his soul an offering for sin, he shall see his seed and he shall prolong his days, and the pleasure of the LORD shall prosper in his hand."* Here is our Jesus, hanging from a tree, not only is He wearing the thorns from the cursed ground upon His head, hanging above Him are the charges for our sin, *"Jesus, King of the Jews."* When the Roman's would crucify someone, they would hang the charges against that person whom they were crucifying above their head so that the public would see the charge and be discouraged from choosing the same path as the one who hung on the cross. In the case of Jesus, He was charged with treason, making Himself out to be a ruler when He was not. Was this not Adam's and the woman's sin? They wanted to be like God, they wanted to know what only He could know and come out from His authority? And is it not our sin? We, who want to rule our own lives, We want to be kings of our own small existence, yet there was Jesus hanging on *our* Cross, dying for *our* charges, made into one giant bruise for *our* healing. He made a way for us through the Cross, a way of hope. And it was at the Cross, the place where the serpent seemingly won the greatest victory that his head was finally crushed. No longer could the venom from his bite poison our lives, it lost all its potency at the Cross. He could still bite, but in Christ there was no longer the sting of death, for Jesus had taken every ounce of our poison upon Himself. First Corinthians 15:55 celebrates this truth with these words," *O death, where is your victory? O death, where is your sting?"*

As we get back to Genesis 3, we see God reinforce the hope that will come through the new life that comes from woman. Just as man will have to fulfill his calling with great frustration, so now woman will have to do the same. *"I will surely multiply your pain in childbearing; in pain you shall bring forth children." (Genesis 3:16a) Even* for those women who do not have children, the reality of these words still work their way through our lives, for every women experiences being a child, as well as other forms of life giving in this world. All of us know what it is to belong to a world in which even the most vulnerable among us, our children, are subjected to great pain and the sting of the helplessness that often accompanies not being able to protect children, or those we seek to give life to, from the brutality in this world. No matter whether it is our own personal experience with giving birth and raising babies, the experience of this pain is real to all of us.

Please, take a moment and share an experience from your own life about this pain, whether as a mother or a woman who has felt the pain of the curse in other ways.

For me, it has been the pain of watching my own children suffer from my own sin, which has caused me the greatest remorse, yet it has also caused me the greatest humility. In so many ways, it has been my role as a mother that has allowed Christ to mold and shape my heart in ways that I might not have allowed Him to otherwise. This momma walks with some bruised heels, but I walk with great hope and great trust in Christ Who holds my right hand and does not let me fall. He is teaching me to grab His grace by force, and it is saving my life and my mind. When I see a manifestation of who I once was, and honestly still struggle not to be anymore, alive and active in my children, it both breaks my heart and humbles me. Yet, I know I have only one place to stand in response and that is in the light of my Savior and Bridegroom. Because He has delivered me from the darkness, I know my only response towards them is to stay in His light, and in so doing, offer them the same thing that He offered to me, a Way out.

Some of the most comforting words in the Bible for me are found in Genesis 3:16b, *"Your desire shall be for your husband, and he shall rule over you."*

You might be wondering how in the world these words can comfort me when they were pronounced as part of a curse; after all, they are spoken to the woman as a direct result of her sin. However, remember at the first of today's lesson I talked about how God's kingdom is an upside down, inside out one? Even in His discipline, we can find great hope.

If I look at these words and attribute them to my earthly husband, I am greatly challenged and can even become resentful. However, in God's amazing grace He has allowed me to see these words in new light, *"Rhonda, your desire shall be for Me, your Husband, and you don't have to worry about making mistakes, just keep giving your heart to Me, for I will over-rule you."*

As I take in these words from my beloved Jesus, I am greatly blessed because in and of myself I know I can't walk this journey that He has called me to. But I find in these words' great assurance that the burden of this journey is on His shoulders. My job is to let Him in my heart, and His job is to rule over me and even my desire to allow Him to do so originates in Him. As I realize this great truth, even my struggle to accept the authority of my earthly husband takes on new light. As I submit to my heavenly Husband, I can delight in allowing Christ in me to make me a woman who will submit to her earthly one.

In His love I can overflow with His Presence and it comes out all around me, blessing others and helping them to see the truth and reality of Jesus.

What about you Beloved? Take a moment and personalize the words from Genesis 3:16b yourself and give yourself time to respond to these precious words below.

____

____

____

____

____

What an amazing privilege we have in being the bride of Christ! My heart is so overwhelmed with thankfulness I can hardly hold it in.

Let's close with a prayer thanking Him for allowing us to become His bride and the one with whom He will share this upside down, inside out Kingdom.

Week 4:
Naked and Not Ashamed

DAY   1

"And the man and his wife were both naked and were not ashamed." (Genesis 2:25)

"Then the eyes of both were opened and they knew that they were naked. And they sewed fig leaves together and made themselves loincloths." (Genesis 3:7)

We talked briefly about the beautiful union between God, man and woman that occurred during the very first wedding ceremony. We often forget that marriage is not only between a man and a woman, but also God. The Creator of all things stands over and watched, as the two became one flesh. Not only does He stand over it, but He also initiates it and enables two to become one.

Today, we will take time to consider the miracle of the marriage that God has given us, not marriage as we define it which is stained by sin and our wrong perceptions and experiences. But marriage as God intended it to be, marriage that enables a man and woman to stand before God and one another, *"naked and not ashamed."*

We spent a lot of time in week 2 discussing the Mikvah: the ceremonial cleansing that a Hebrew bride takes part in on becoming a Ka'lah (called out one, bride).

Please, record below what you can remember about the Mikah from week 2.

____

____

____

____

____

The Mikvah was one of her first acts once her groom left to go and prepare a place for her. It was symbolic of her washing away her old identity and coming to life in her new one. She would usually have at least one attendant with her to not only witness her re-birth and to attend to her needs but also to help ensure that the cleansing water touched every part of her body. This was truly a time for her to be naked and not ashamed. Literally, every single part of her body that had been exposed to her old life was to be washed away in the living waters that the Mikvah provided.

There are a few verses that correlate with our Mikvah. Please, look up the following verses and record your thoughts about how they tie in with Mikvah.

Hebrews 10:19-22

____

____

____

____

____

Ephesians 5:26

____

____

____

____

____

John 13:5

____

____

____

____

____

Revelation 22:14-17

____

____

____

____

____

In these verses we see the wonder of how, even before we can understand who Christ is as our Husband, He is already busy playing the part. He is washing us through the curtain of His flesh, cleansing us with the water of His Word, washing our feet of all sin, and even allowing us to be blessed by washing our robes in His righteousness in the River of Life. Long before we had any idea what Mikvah was, He had become our place of cleansing.

One aspect of the Mikvah we have not gone over yet, has to do with the need for the bride to continue Mikvah all throughout her married life. Her first Mikvah happened at the time of her wedding, and as we discussed earlier was symbolic of her washing away her old identity. However, once she became a bride and a wife, each month after her cycle, she would be required to participate in Mikvah again. At the first sight of blood, a bride was considered unclean and therefore unable to have any relations with her husband. In order to become clean again, she must complete her cycle and enter the waters of Mikvah. As she washes each time in her monthly routine, she is called to examine herself and to be renewed and conformed more and more into her new identity as wife, mother, and daughter of God. It is actually very beautiful, and in it we can see God's tender desire for His daughter to know and understand the pricelessness that exists in her awareness of who she is as His own.

What about you, as you learn more about Mikvah and what it entails, what are your opinions? Please, share below.

____

____

____

____

____

While I might find the process of Mikvah beautiful, what I find most beautiful about it is the way that Christ enables us to have Mikvah anytime we want. There is no more ritual involved, for He has made a way for us to come to Him any time we want by carving out a place through His own flesh that enables us to be clean before Him.

In fact, we already are completely clean before Him, however there is still one part of us that can become hung up in the flesh. Let's look again at Hebrews 10:22, *"let us draw near with a true heart in full assurance of faith, with our hearts sprinkled clean from an evil conscience and our bodies washed with pure water."* Before Christ, our conscience is what often kept us from God. It condemned us because, even though we may have fought it and denied it tooth and nail, deep inside we all know what we are. There in something in us that knows that we are unclean and unable to stand before the living and loving God. Like a vampire running away from the sunlight that will cause him to disappear, we run from the Son, feeling that His Light will overtake us and cause us to become lost in Him. Until that day when the weight of our darkness renders us powerless, and we have no more options left than to surrender to the Light. And when we do, we realize that as our darkness flees, we are not lost, as we had feared, instead we are found!

And as we begin to walk in His Light, our hearts become more and more attuned and uncomfortable with darkness. Instead of it being our covering as it once was, it has now become our enemy and the one thing that keeps His light from burning as brightly as it can in us. Perhaps 1 John best describes this relationship between His light and our darkness (which comes to bear witness in our conscience).

Please, read the scripture below and then draw a diagram or picture to represent the relationship between our darkness and His Light.

1 John 1:5-10

"This is the message we have heard from him and proclaim to you, that God is light, and in him is no darkness at all. If we say we have fellowship with him while we walk in darkness, we lie and do not practice the truth. But if we walk in the light as He is in the light, we have fellowship with one another, and the blood of Jesus His Son cleanses us from all sin. And if we say we have no sin, we deceive ourselves, and the truth is not in us. If we confess our sins, He is faithful and just to forgive our sins and to cleanse us from all unrighteousness. If we say we have not sinned, we make him a liar, and his word is not in us."

Beloved, your Mikvah, Jesus, is right there with you, towel wrapped around His waist, ready and willing to wash away anything that keeps your heart from fully belonging to Him. On the Cross, He paid for every step of this journey with you. He paid for the privilege to be the one to wash away every stain of darkness that enters His beloved, which is you. Sometimes we feel either too worthless to make maintaining His Light in us a priority, or even more painful, we feel that He is too worthless to make maintaining His Light in us a priority. We allow the world's tide to wash us away into the *ocean of whatever*. But He waits there with the bowl of life-giving water to wash away even our filthiest sins.

Let's close our time together today by allowing our Mikvah, Jesus, to wash away whatever lies between your heart and His. Like the very first wedding day, let's determine to live out what God created and let no man (even you) separate.

"And the man and his wife were both naked and were not ashamed." (Genesis 2:25)

DAY 2

"Then the eyes of both were opened and they knew that they were naked. And they sewed fig leaves together and made themselves loincloths." (Genesis 3:7)

Beloved, yesterday we looked more deeply into how Jesus is our Mikvah. He provided all that we will ever need to be ceremonially clean by taking all our darkness to the Cross and giving us His righteousness. Today, we look at an example from His Word about what this actually looks like. In John 4 we see a perfect example of Mikvah happening right before our eyes.

Please read John 4:1-34 and answer the questions that follow

In verse 6, what is the physical condition of Jesus?

____

____

____

____

____

In verses 7-11, we see an interchange happen between Jesus and the Samaritan woman, who initiated this interchange? What does Jesus say that He would offer her?

____

____

____

____

____

Out of all the chapters in the Bible, this is one of my favorites. I just relate well to the woman at the well. I have been her, felt the rejection that she must have felt and the desperation in her heart that longed for that "right man" who would finally love her and fill that gaping hole in her heart. And finally, still thirsty, she finds herself having gone through disappointment after disappointment, hope after hope, she decides to trade in her dream of ever quenching her thirst for a chance at mere survival. It is here, ironically, at a well where she encounters the One who will forever quench her thirst.

Here, beloved, we see one of the criteria in place for a filling (or a washing) to take place. She was **thirsty**.

We may come to Christ for other reasons, but we will not be filled with Him until we are thirsty.

When was the last time you were really thirsty? It could be physical or spiritual. Describe the circumstances below and how your thirst was quenched.

____

____

____

____

____

In verses 12-14, we see this divine exchange taking a turn as Jesus introduces to her what He is able to provide for her.

What is it that He can provide and what does it do?

____

____

____

____

____

I just love verse 15, He is doing His darn best to describe to her something deeper and more meaningful than water, however all she can see is the chance to not have to come and draw water again from this well. We know from observing the time at which she came (noon), that she did not come when the other women came to draw water. For most Hebrew women, getting water was their first task to attend to in the morning. It was also a social occasion, a chance for them to begin their day with an encouraging word, or to perhaps take in the village gossip. We can easily assume that this woman did not want to be around the other women. Perhaps, as we look deeper into her past, we can see how easily she may have often been the subject of village gossip. Even if she weren't, her own shame gave her ample opportunity to feel like she deserved to be.

Sometimes our deepest shame comes from those needs that we have and seek filling for. We become vulnerable to our need, and finally give into it and immediately the shame comes to convict us and isolate us, leaving us thirstier than we were before. Each of us can look into a part of our heart and see a weakness or vulnerability that we have. It is so often these deepest needs that are most also associated with our deepest shame.

This, beloved, goes all the way back to the beginning. *"Then the eyes of both were opened and they knew that they were naked. And they sewed fig leaves together and made themselves loincloths." (Genesis 3:7)* Before the fruit could hit the ground, man and woman had a new reality open to them. Their first response to one another after sin entered the world was to hide, from each other and from God.

"They made themselves loincloths," they covered over up those places that were most sacred and represented the greatest vulnerability. The woman at the well had opened up her place of greatest vulnerability to at least six men because her thirst was greater than her fear of being exposed. Have you ever been there beloved? **Have you ever been so thirsty for an unmet need that you were even willing to make a fool out of yourself to have your need met?** If so, you are in good company sweet one. There are so many reasons why I love Jesus, but one of them is that He never makes me feel like a fool, even though He knows I've been one. He never tires of turning my ashes into a crown of beauty and then telling me how precious and lovely I am with that crown on my head. Just like the woman at the well who was drawn to the well because of her thirst, yet walked away with so much more, **Jesus will use the areas of our greatest defeat to bring us into our greatest victory.**

As we go on to read verses 16-34, we see how the rest of this story goes. Jesus tells her the truth about herself, and she is exposed, laid bare before Him. The very thing she tried to avoid, by going to the well at noon, is laid out before her. We can see her trying to cover herself by changing the subject in verses 19-20.

How do you most often respond when you are exposed?

Beloved, in Christ you never have to be worried about hiding. In Him you are safe to open and expose yourself before Him in deepest vulnerability. All of us need a safe place to hide in this world, and Jesus has provided it and even came for our places of deepest shame and insecurity. Just as He did for the woman at the well, so He does for us. He gives us a safe place to be exposed and then He covers our truth with the truth about Himself.

We see this beautifully portrayed in verses 21-26, just after that uncomfortable exchange before, He opens the door for her to see that He is offering her a safe place to be found in Him. He goes on to tell her that He is seeking those who will worship Him in Spirit and in Truth. And then He introduces Himself to her as the Messiah. Just as a bride washes her identity away in the cleansing waters of Mikvah, so this woman is invited to wash herself away in the revelation of Jesus.

The story never says how the woman responds to this revelation in word, but we know based on her actions that she accepted this offer. Verses 28-29 say, *"So the woman left her water jar and went away into town and said to the people, "Come, see a man who told me all that I ever did. Can this be the Christ?"*

As I read this my heart saw something new, in verse 25 the woman is talking about the Messiah and says to Jesus, *"...When he comes, he will tell us all things."* And as I see her sweet words in verse 29, *"Come, see a man who told me all that I ever did..."* I can't help but notice that she already had knowledge about the Messiah before she met Him, but it seems her knowledge was in a general sense. It was as if she had believed that He was coming one day, and then she would begin to understand things that she could not until He came. When Jesus announced to her that He is the Messiah, she had to take responsibility for the truth He was sharing with her about herself and Him, right then in that moment she had to decide if she was willing to stand before Him naked and no longer be ashamed.

 I love it that the last we see of her, she is running to the people who she had just been hiding from. Those are the actions of a woman who is made new, a woman who is clean, a woman who is no longer ashamed, a woman who was no longer thirsty.

DAY 3

"Then the LORD God said, 'It is not good that the man should be alone, I will make a helper fit for him.'" (Genesis 2:18)

"And the Lord made for Adam and for his wife garments of skins and clothed them." (Genesis 3:21)

Yesterday, we spent precious time with the Samaritan woman at the well. A woman who allowed Christ to become not only her Mikvah, but also her wellspring of living water. The beautiful thing about Jesus is that He not only cleanses us from the outside, but also from the inside out, while at the same time quenching our great thirst for more than we see and experience in this world. We will spend today looking at just one more example of how our beloved Husband provides for us. We will begin from Genesis 2:18, *"Then the LORD God said, 'It is not good that the man should be alone, I will make a helper fit for him.'"* Before woman was ever created, God saw the need for her. Before Adam had any clue that he was alone in the garden, God saw the need and already had a plan to provide. From the very beginning we see His providence taking place, a sweet assurance for all of us who so often need to be reminded that He sees, He knows, and He will provide.

Let's take a moment here and share a need in our lives. What is something you perceive that you need and may be waiting on God to provide? It might be something tangible, or even something intangible such as an answer to a question that has been on your heart for a long time.

____

____

____

____

____

Beloved, I am not sure what your need is, but I am sure that God knows and just as He did for Adam, He will provide.

Let's get back to Genesis 2 and read verses 18-22 together and then answer the questions below.

In verses 19, how does it say that God responded to His acknowledgement that it was not good for man to be alone?

____

____

____

____

____

Does His response seem a little off to you? If God saw that it was not good for Adam to be alone, why didn't He just create a woman and bring her to him right away? Write your thoughts below.

____

____

____

____

____

If we look closely here, we can see a huge hint about one of the ways God works in our lives. We can assume that He knew that He was going to make a helper for Adam, however before He did; He allowed Adam's heart to be prepared first. Through naming the animals, Adam is not only able to see with his own two eyes the reality of his predicament, he is able to experience in his heart the sense of loneliness that comes when one understands that they are alone in the world, that there is no one like them to share their life and experiences with. Adam watched the animals; male and female make families and enjoy one another in ways that we have never seen. Before the fall, the whole earth was alive and full of God's glory. Death and decay had never touched any part of the world. Everything was completely alive and vibrant with God's breath in and on everything. It was a world that we cannot even imagine. Everything was completely as it should be, except for this one missing piece.

It is ironic that after each day of creation in Genesis 1, we see over and over again that after each phase of creation is done, God says these words, *"and God saw that it was good."* The very first place we see Him saying that something is not good is when it deals with man being alone. The next words we see coming from God are these, *"I will make a helper fit for him."* In human eyes we understand the word, *"make"* to involve an action on one's part in direct response to what one sees as needing, for instance, we need to "make" our bed because we have a desire for it to appear nice and neat, or we might "make" a peanut butter and jelly sandwich because we are hungry. **However, we often see God's first action in responding to a need to be one of causing someone to be awakened to the need long before any "making" appears**. His ways are so much higher than ours and His ways always involve the heart.

We can all think of examples in our own lives when we thought we needed something and for one reason or other, God did not allow that need to be met. At least not in the way that we thought it needed to be. **Like He sent Adam out to name the animals in an attempt to recognize what was lacking, so He sends us out on a journey in order to help us recognize what is truly lacking in our own lives**. And just as Adam must have done as he named the animals, we enter circumstance after circumstance, experience after experience thinking, "maybe this one will fulfill what is lacking." A deep sense of longing sets in and we begin to realize just as Adam must have, that there is not a helper suitable for us.

As women, so often we have been like the woman at the well. Some of us, like me and like the Samaritan woman, have tried man after man looking for the one that would fill our need, while others try on different versions of themselves in an attempt to become something more. We tend to either look at a different version of our self to fill the need, or at a different version of someone outside of us to fill the need. Either way, just as Adam did, we all eventually end up in the same place, in the place where our hearts are broken because we realize that there is no helper fit for us.

It is at that moment of desperation, of true awakening to what our deepest longing is for that God is able to finally begin His process of making a helper that fits us.

Beloved, Jesus is the only One Who truly "fits" you and me. No amount of sinful flesh can fill the empty place in our heart. God loves you and I so much that He sends us out on this journey, this wedding ceremony and gives us so much, yet withholds the one thing we need most in this life until our hearts are awakened to the awareness that what we need most, we do not have. Part of His provision in giving us Christ as our beloved Bridegroom, is in giving us the journey in awakening to our deep need for Him. He is the only One who is big enough to cover even our most shameful experiences, yet at the same time small enough to get into the tiny, intricate places in our hearts that no one with skin possibly understand.

And He provides. Just as He sent Adam into a deep sleep and took the rib from His side, so He sent Jesus into a deep sleep on the Cross and out of His side came the blood and water that redeemed us all.

As you look back over your journey to know Christ, what are some of the places or circumstances that God allowed you to experience in order to awaken to your need for Him?

____

____

____

____

____

My heart overflows with gratitude for our God Who knows our needs in ways that we can't begin to see or imagine. As we look at the following verse, I am renewed with a sense of awe at how precious our Father's love is for us. *"And the LORD made for Adam and for his wife garments of skins and clothed them." (Genesis 3:21)* The very first death we see occurs after the fall happened when God killed Adam's beloved, innocent animals in order to make clothes for he and Eve to wear.

The garments of fig leaves would not suffice to cover them up, they were clothed in what represented sacrifice. There had to be innocent blood to cover their guilt.

Just as God provided a helper fit for Adam in the form of a woman, so in this one act we see the actions of our Lord already pointing to the only true Helper fit for us, who would wear our cross in order to cover all of our guilt once and for all.

"Then the LORD God said, 'It is not good that the man should be alone, I will make a helper fit for him.'" (Genesis 2:18)

Let's close today's lesson thanking Jesus for providing the One true Helper that is fit just for us. Please, personalize the scripture above and close in a prayer of gratitude.

"Then the LORD God said, 'It is not good that the man should be alone, I will make a helper fit for him.'" (Genesis 2:18)

DAY 4

"When the wine had run out, the mother of Jesus said to him, 'They have no wine.'" (John 2:3)

"For I tell you that from now on I will not drink of the fruit of the vine until the kingdom of God comes." (Luke 22:18)

If you have never noticed the divine romance that we see in scripture, I pray that your eyes will be opened to see it today. We will close out this week by looking at a wedding. Is it any wonder that our beloved Jesus began His earthly ministry at a wedding? And beloved, as we enter the fullness of Him in glory, our story will pick right up with our wedding with Him in heaven.

Please, do me the honor of meeting me in John 2 as we look into the wedding at Cana.

Let's read verses 1-12 together and then answer the questions below.

In verses 3-4, we see an interchange happening between Jesus and His mom, please, note below what the situation is.

____

____

____

____

____

In verse 6 what does it mention the jars being used for? How many jars are there?

____

____

____

____

____

In verses 7 and 9, who does Jesus includes in this first miracle?

____

____

____

____

I must admit, I have been a little confused at the first part of this account. After all, shouldn't Jesus be the one to decide when He will begin His earthly ministry? How like it for a mom to try to intervene and even boss around the Messiah! Some parts of the Bible are almost comical in how we see God use humans in the greatest story ever told. However, as I look upon this story again, I am filled with the knowledge of God's sovereign choice of a wedding from which to begin the redemption of His people. It is almost as if to highlight to us, His Bride, about who it is Jesus is coming for. With these words, *"they have no more wine." (John 2:3).* Although it may appear that Mary is the one getting this ball rolling, we can be assured that no detail concerning Christ's ministry is overlooked. His mother may have been the one to draw attention to the need, but Jesus was the One who chose to obey in complete accordance with His Father's will to fulfill it. Ancient Hebrew weddings were huge events, often lasting for days or maybe even weeks. As we learned earlier in the series, there are two parts to the wedding. The wedding that Jesus is attending now is the second part. We can assume that the bridegroom had built his bride her chamber, and she had endured her time of waiting (her betrothal). She had kept her lamp in the window and at a time she did not expect, her groom had come for her, lifting her up into a liter. And she had been lifted into the cart and carried back to fulfill the second half of her wedding, where the bride and groom would consummate the marriage and then have a feast to celebrate the fulfillment of the wedding covenant. During this celebration, wine and food was served extravagantly.

For there to be no more wine would have been not only a damper on the party, but also a huge embarrassment to the bride and groom, as well as the parents.

In light of Jesus' ministry, this miracle still seems to be a bit small. It is not until we dig a bit deeper that we can grasp the amazing beauty and even the wonder at how Jesus went out of His way to let His Bride know He had been thinking about her from the very beginning.

Before we go deeper, let's take a moment to reflect on what your thoughts are about why He chose a wedding to begin His earthly ministry?

____

____

____

____

____

Verse 6 says, "*Now there were six stone water jars there for the Jewish rites of purification, each holding twenty or thirty gallons.*" My eyes first stop on the word "**stone**", as we learned in previous teaching, when God first gave His covenant to His people, He wrote it upon tablets of stone. In Ezekiel 11:19 we see God giving a glimpse of what He will do in establishing this new covenant, His wedding contract, with His Bride. It says, "*And I will give them one heart, and a new spirit I will put within them. I will remove the heart of stone from their flesh and give them a heart of flesh*" As we consider that these jars were made of stone, we can compare them to the law that God gave to Moses in the 10 commandments, the law that the Jews could not seem to keep. Just as Adam had to name the animals in order to be awakened to his greater need for a helper, God provided a way for His people to see what they were lacking in order for them to be awakened to the Helper that He was sending to them in the form of His Son, Jesus.

The next word that stands out to me is the word, **purification**. The Hebrews would wash before eating, the water that had been in these jars had been used to make the people who attended the wedding ceremonially clean, which enabled them to take part in the wedding festivities. As we first encounter these jars, they are empty; the water had been poured out and used up.

Beloved, can you see it? Do you see yourself in that emptied out, stone water jar?

____

____

____

____

____

Below are some stone water jars, take a moment and write in some of the ways in which you have tried to fill yourself up.

Here are some of my ways: Relationships (both romantic and friendships), education, career, family, religious activities, fixation on physical health

Whether we are trying to become "filled" or whether we are trying to become clean, Jesus is the only answer to our dilemma. Hearts of stone cannot be changed by what it holds on the inside; they can only be exchanged so that they will be able to hold new desires for the filling, and new awareness of righteousness for the cleaning. Jesus came to do both. When He married you beloved, He took your heart of stone and exchanged it for His heart of flesh, *"And I will give them one heart, and a new spirit I will pout within them. I will remove the heart of stone from their flesh and give them a heart of flesh" (Ezekiel 11:19)*

I don't know about you beloved, but I love that the very first people who get to see the wonder of who Jesus is are the servants. Verse 7 and verse 9 both testify that not only are they the ones who were asked the fill these jars with water that He would later turn into wine, but they also were the ones who got to share this wine with the master of the feast. The same is true with us beloved. Jesus assures us in *John 12:26, "Whoever serves me must follow me; and where I am, my servant also will be. My Father will honor the one who serves me."*

Let's close in prayer thanking Jesus for not only exchanging our hearts of stone for His heart of flesh and cleansing us once and for all from all unrighteousness, but also inviting us to do what only He can do in offering ourselves to become His servants in this world.

DAY 5

"and he said to him, everyone serves the good wine first, and when people have drunk freely, then the poor wine. But you have kept the good wine until now." (John 2:10)

"And likewise the cup after they had eaten, saying 'This cup that is poured out for you is the new covenant in my blood.'" (Luke 22:20)

We are spending this last day back at the wedding in Cana, to examine once again the very first of Jesus' signs once He began His earthly ministry. We spent yesterday examining the stone jars that had been filled with water for the ceremonial cleansing of the wedding guests. These are the same six jars that Jesus would ask the servants to fill with water, with which He would turn to wine.

Before we go further into our lesson today, let's start by remembering why this miracle was needed in the first place.

Look at John 2:3, what was the precursor to this miracle?

____

____

____

____

____

So often we believe that a precursor for a miracle to take place is great faith, and perhaps amazing humility. We often might even falsely believe that for a miracle to happen, there must be someone who is worthy of experiencing one. This leads us to believe that we are not deserving of a miracle to happen in our own lives for we so often feel that we don't measure up, and therefore are disqualified from experiencing the miracle of Jesus in our own lives. We even see this in the groom's father who was hosting the wedding, he does not even acknowledge his need to anyone. Perhaps, like we so often are, he is so embarrassed and terrified at his lack of wine that he just decides to hide his head in the sand and hope that somehow no one will notice.

Only one thing happens when we do that…**nothing**! We see Mary, the only one who was willing to address the need and to bring the need into the light of Christ. She doesn't tell Jesus what to do, but simply leaves the predicament in His lap.

"they have no wine." Beloved, what is the place in your life right now where you simply have no more wine; you are bone dry in what you know you need to carry on?

____

____

____

____

____

Let's take a moment here, pull our heads out of the sand and acknowledge our dilemma to Christ.

We do not need to be a super hero in the faith to experience the miracle of Christ. He is Emmanuel, Christ with us. All that He needs for us to experience the filling that only He can do is our willingness to acknowledge our need to Him.

In your opinion, what keeps us from bringing our needs to Him?

____

____

____

____

____

I am curious to find out what your answers are. In my own life, it seems that I often view Jesus as my last resort instead of my ever-present supply. I try everything I can do in my own strength, and wisdom, and when that runs out, ask Jesus for help. In all honesty, I think that I simply do not know how to accept His help so much of the time. So busy trying to dissect all the reasons to explain away my thirst, I do not often do the one easy thing that is required in simply saying, *"Jesus, I am thirsty."* As I grow closer and more reliant upon Him, I am beginning to not only experience the wonder of what it is to be filled up in Him, but even more amazing the wonder of Him becoming my ever-present supply.

Do you believe it is possible for Jesus to literally become your Wellspring of Living Water? If so, what does that look like in your life?

I love that Jesus takes the time to ask the servant to fill these empty jars. He could have just caused wine to suddenly appear in these huge water jars, yet He asks them to join Him in His miracle. We see this principle carried out all through His earthly ministry. He does not only become our Savior, but He also invites others to come along with Him, to experience Him and to be entrusted with the story of who He is to us, and eventually they become the very first ones to share the good news, the news that God has come for us. Even today beloved, He is still inviting you and I to join in the wonder of being used by Him.

As I ponder what this looks like, I can't help but relate more to those empty stone jars. So cold and useless, all poured out, and then someone with human hands drops a drink into me, they do the only thing they can do by trying to fill the emptiness in my heart up with water, and then He turns it into wine. He takes their offering into His hands and blesses it and somehow what was only meant to quench a thirst becomes so much more. It becomes the very thing that brings a joy that cannot be experienced except in the heart of one who knows Jesus. He turns our water into wine.

In yesterday's lesson, we wrote down some of the ways in which we try to fill ourselves in this world, as well as some of the ways we try to clean ourselves up. Today, let's give praise to Jesus as we acknowledge before Him ways in which He has turned our water into wine.

In the stone jars below, please, record areas of thirst in your life where you have seen Jesus come in and not only fill you but take the water and turn into inexpressible joy.

If you have not experienced this, why not ask Him to turn your water into wine today.

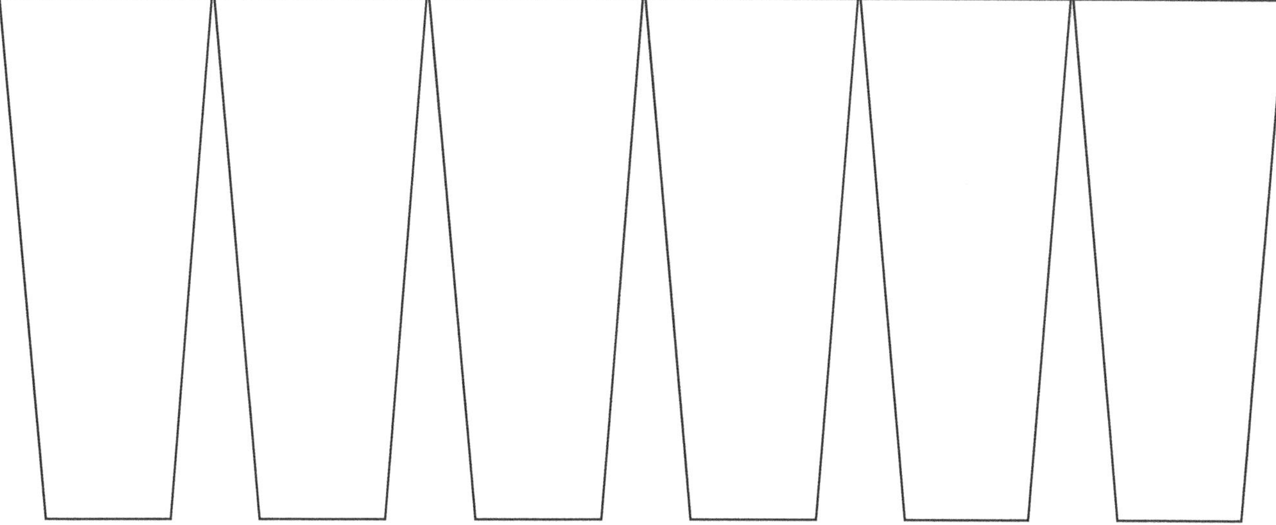

I can't help but imagine the look on the bridegroom's father's face as he heard these words come from the master of the ceremony, *"and he said to him, everyone serves the good wine first, and when people have drunk freely, then the poor wine. But you have kept the good wine until now." (John 2:10)* I can just imagine that as he saw the master of the feast coming toward him, he began to tremble with fear, knowing that his greatest shame was about to become public knowledge; he did not have enough. I did not know until recently exactly how big of a deal it was to run out of wine at a wedding. The guests who were attending could actually take the bridegroom to court over not having what he had promised to provide. And here he was, caught, just like Isaac was when his father Abraham had bound him to the altar. And to his amazement, his moment of greatest fear becomes his moment of greatest honor and even wonder. His greatest lack was the precursor to his greatest joy. So, it is with us, beloved. We are all bound, caught in our sin, in all the hundreds of ways we try to hide our lack from the world. And yet, just as God provided for Abraham and Isaac on the mountain. So, He does for us, *"behold, behind him was a ram, caught in the thicket by his horns." (Genesis 22:13).* The lamb was already caught beloved. That moment or that thing you fear being exposed, He already bore and exposed Himself to it over 2000 years ago on the Cross. Just as Abraham did, look behind you beloved, He is already there. Caught in the thicket of your mess and mine, waiting for us to acknowledge Him and apply His blood over our hearts.

"And likewise, the cup after they had eaten, saying, 'This cup that is poured out for you is the new covenant in my blood.' (Luke 22:20) Do you see, right here beloved? His hand is held out to you right now, offering you the wine! Taste and see that He is good!

Let's close today by taking a moment to drink from the cup that He is holding out to us right now.

I am going to begin this prayer and want you to end it however you see fit, let the joy of His wine overflow in your heart.

"Jesus, thank-You for being enough for me, thank-You for giving me the permission to not be enough in this world, and not only giving me the permission to be lacking but also giving me the joy of being filled in You, as well as being the one who gets to taste and see the wonder of Your wine, Amen.

Week 5:
Saying Yes to the Dress

DAY 1

"But when the king came in to look at the guests, he saw there a man who had no wedding garment. And he said to him, 'Friend, how did you get in here without a wedding garment?' And he was speechless." (Matthew 22:11-12)

"The one who conquers will be clothed thus in white garments, and I will never blot out his name out of the book of life. I will confess his name before my Father and before His angels." (Revelation 3:5)

Beloved, we have been to some beautiful places with Jesus in our journey with Him so far. And now we are turning a corner towards the second half of the wedding. Up to this point, we have observed many aspects of our wedding with Christ that have already taken place, for He has already married us, and we are still in the process of awaiting His arrival for the second part of our wedding to Him to take place. As He said in John 14, *"I go to prepare a place for you."* And again, in John 14, *"I will come again and will take you to myself, that where I am you may be also."* In His Kingdom calendar, we sit literally between these two statements right now, awaiting His return to take us to that place that He has prepared for us. For the remainder of our study, we will be looking at what takes place during that second part of the wedding. As always in scripture, even though we are looking at future events, there are so many applications to our lives now.

Let's go ahead and dive right in as we discuss in Hebrew terms, what it means to "say yes to the dress."

Meet me in Matthew 22, and let's read verses 1-14 together.

I don't know about you but being underdressed at a wedding would surely seem embarrassing enough to me. However, we see in scripture that this person received a severe punishment for showing up without the proper attire, not only severe, but eternal!

Let's look deeper into what Jesus was showing us in this parable.

Please, take some time to respond to the following questions.

Go back to chapter 21 and list the subtitles that are found there. (Hint, the first one is The Triumphant Entry).

To better understand what scripture is saying, we must always keep it in context. For instance, your mom saying, "we need to talk," when you are thirteen and have not obeyed her in keeping your room clean means something completely different from when you are thirty and you know that she has just been given a serious health diagnosis. The Bible is God's Word, it is His conversation to us, and as we investigate the context here, we see that Jesus has just entered Jerusalem for the final time. He knows His time here on earth is coming to an end, we don't see Him displaying any huge miracles at this point. He is telling stories, parables in hopes that they will help His bride to recognize the love story that is occurring right there in her midst, the greatest love story ever told, God coming to redeem His lost love.

As we look closer into the parable of the wedding feast, we must keep in the mind the two parables just before this one, for they all share a common theme.

Take time to read over Matthew 21:28-46, and after doing so, record your thoughts about the common theme those two parables share with Matthew 22:1-14, the parable of the wedding feast.

Did you catch it? At this point Jesus had quite the audience, there are many who were hanging on His every word, in hopes that what He said might apply to them, that they might find life in Him. And much like today, there were others who were listening to Him for a very different reason. They wanted to catch Him in His words, they had already determined in their hearts and minds that they knew more than Him and therefore were looking for reasons to justify their own preconceived ideas about who He claimed to be. Essentially, there were those who received Him, and those who did not. He kept them both spellbound with His truth, but His truth only appeared to be Good News to one group of people. This group found hope that they might have a chance to be welcomed and loved by God. This news was almost too good to be true, for up until that point, the God of Abraham, Isaac, and Jacob, the God who had displayed miraculous power, and the only God Who had shown Himself to be alive and strong in might and power on behalf of His people, had been off limits to anyone who was not Jewish. A truth that, many Jews were willing to reject at the cost of Truth, Himself. For them, the exclusivity of being God's chosen mattered more than God, Himself. Oh, how I pray that never becomes us. It is hard for us who have had access to Jesus our whole lives to believe, but what seems so harsh right here in these parables is the greatest news in the world to us, the gentiles. With the rejection of His own people, came the invitation to us, we who never stood a chance, who never had access to God before. He was being brought out, so that we could have the chance to be brought in.

Let's close in prayer thanking Jesus for becoming the stone that the builders rejected to become our Chief cornerstone.

DAY 2

"But when the king came in to look at the guests, he saw there a man who had no wedding garment. And he said to him, 'Friend, how did you get in here without a wedding garment?' And he was speechless." (Matthew 22:11-12)

"The one who conquers will be clothed thus in white garments, and I will never blot out his name out of the book of life. I will confess his name before my Father and before His angels." (Revelation 3:5)

Yesterday, we looked at the theme of what Jesus was sharing with the people as He entered the last leg of His earthly journey. Today, we will home in on what He shared in Matthew 22 through the parable of the wedding feast.

Let's begin by looking over Matthew 22:1-14 again and then answering the questions below.

In verse 2, what does Jesus say He is going to compare through His telling of this parable?

____

____

____

____

____

Also, in verse 2, who do we see is getting married?

____

____

____

____

____

In verses 3-6, we see the King sending out servants to announce to those who were invited to come to the wedding, based on these verses, what is the response?

____

____

____

____

____

Verses 5-6 give us some insight into why they rejected the kings offer, based on how you see others responding to Christ today, what parallels can you find between how these people responded and how we respond to Christ today.

____

____

____

____

____

I find it convicting as I really ponder the above question. I know that I have accepted the King's offer; I have become His bride. However, becoming His bride is not just a onetime occurrence. It is something that I need to surrender to each day, sometimes multiple times a day. It is an identity I am realizing more and more as I go. It is easy to glance over this parable and see how I fit into the story and forget how it does not apply to me anymore. Each day, Jesus comes for me. Every moment He is still inviting me in. In essence, He is saying, "I have prepared a feast for you, won't you come in and dine with Me?" And if I am honest, there have been so many times that I have been like those in verse 5 who, *"paid no attention and went off..."*

This is important beloved, because we can't miss the moments in the here and now that He is giving to us. We can't place the "I already know Jesus," band-aid over our lives and miss the gravity of what He truly came for; a living, moving, breathing relationship with His bride. If He wanted a bride that merely adhered to a to-do list, He could have had that. He wanted a bride to love and one that was able to love Him back. Just as earthly relationships require an investment, so does this heavenly one. Each day He still comes for us and beckons us to turn aside and pay attention to Him, to allow Him to love us and to allow Him to empower us to love Him in return.

Considering where you are with Him right now, what has been your response to Him coming for you? Are you sensitive and responsive to Him or, like the people mentioned in the parable do you often, "pay no attention and go off?"

____

____

____

____

____

Beloved, I must encourage you. The fact that you are even here right now is a great sign that you are turning your heart towards Him. You are dining with your Beloved, and I know that He is head over heels in love with you!

Let's take a moment and close our time together in prayer, asking Jesus to help us become more sensitive to His calling out to us, and that we might respond.

DAY 3

"But when the king came in to look at the guests, he saw there a man who had no wedding garment. And he said to him, 'Friend, how did you get in here without a wedding garment?' And he was speechless." (Matthew 22:11-12)

"The one who conquers will be clothed thus in white garments, and I will never blot out his name out of the book of life. I will confess his name before my Father and before His angels." (Revelation 3:5)

I find myself pondering Matthew 22:5, where it says, *"But they paid no attention and went off..."* As I pray and ask Jesus why it is that we are so prone to go our own way considering what He has to offer us, I can sense Him highlighting this one word, the word *"pay."* I will admit, I love shopping! I love the whole process of examining an item, whether it be something for my house, a piece of clothing, or a gift for a friend or relative. I love the process of searching for that one item that speaks to me; however, there are times when, no matter how loudly an item may be speaking, one look at the price tag says all I need to hear. I simply can't afford the cost.

Considering all Christ has given us, there is really nothing left that we can give Him outside of this one thing, our attention. It is the one command that we are given by God Himself more than once, and it is the only thing that Jesus lets us pay for.

Let's take a moment and look at some of these commands, look up the following verses and record what stands out to you about them below.

Zechariah 1:3-5

____

____

____

____

____

Matthew 17:5

____

____

____

____

____

Mark 9:7

____

____

____

____

____

Luke 9:35

____

____

____

____

____

At this point, you may be thinking, "Rhonda, what in the world does any of this have to do with the wedding theme?" but hang with me here, beloved, because to get dressed for this wedding we must first examine ourselves.

The Greek word used for *listen* in the above verses is *Akouo*. It is a verb, and it means to hear, to give audience to, to understand, and my favorite part of the definition, *to give in to*. In a literal sense, we are to actively give in to what Jesus has to say. **Sometimes it seems so much easier to acknowledge Jesus as a noun, but He requires us to be a verb.** Everything about Him is active, and His Life is to become our life. It is not about having a quiet time, although it would be impossible to truly listen to Jesus without having any time to allow Him to speak to us. But my prayer is that both you and I will allow Him to become so real and alive in us that, at any point in our lives, throughout our days and moments, He might be able to grab our attention and ask us to come away with Him, to pay attention to Him. **Right there in the middle of the hundreds of decisions we make each day, and the countless ways that we spend our time and energy, what could our lives become if we simply obeyed the wish of God for us to pay attention to His Son?**

Please, join me as we close in prayer.

Jesus, how we need you. We live in the midst of a world that is so stimulating. It seems that the one thing we can give to you is the one thing that is hardest for us to grab hold of, and that is our attention. Please, help us Jesus, to give You what You ask, and to pay attention to You. Help us throughout every moment to rest in Who You are so that we might be able to stay in Your presence. Amen

DAY 4

"But when the king came in to look at the guests, he saw there a man who had no wedding garment. And he said to him, 'Friend, how did you get in here without a wedding garment?' And he was speechless." (Matthew 22:11-12)

"The one who conquers will be clothed thus in white garments, and I will never blot out his name out of the book of life. I will confess his name before my Father and before His angels." (Revelation 3:5)

Okay ladies, here is the moment we have been waiting for all week! We are finally going to get to the part where we talk about getting dressed for our wedding!

Let's glance back through Matthew 22:1-14. Then answer the questions below.

In what verse is the word "garment" first mentioned?

____

____

____

____

____

What is the situation? What is happening in this parable to the man who was not wearing a garment?

____

____

____

____

____

At this point you may be wondering what the big deal is about the wedding garment. In ancient Hebrew culture, the father of the groom would provide wedding garments for not only the wedding party to wear, but, if he were very wealthy, he would provide these garments for every guest to wear as well. They were white and were worn over the clothes. Not only did they symbolize the purity of the bride and groom, as guests, they were a symbol of agreement with the wedding. If you were not wearing the garment that was provided for you, in essence, you were saying, I do not agree that this wedding should take place. Remember that, according to the Ketubah, the bride was completely under the canopy of her husband's responsibility once the first part of the wedding had taken place. Also, the father of the groom was the one who had given approval for the second part of the wedding to begin. When he said, "it is time, go get your bride," he was giving his complete approval for the second part of the wedding to take place. We can assume, that under his inspection, everything was perfect. As the overseer of his son, he had been given the responsibility to not only ensure that the bridal chamber was ready for the bride's homecoming, but also that his son was ready as well. For someone to not approve of this wedding was a great affront, not only to the bride and groom, but also to the authority of the father of the groom. It is easy to read through this and see the father of the groom as responding too harshly to this man who showed up at the wedding and was simply underdressed. However, in better understanding of Hebrew culture at the time, we can see that no one in the wedding innocently came undressed. This person had either not been invited, and therefore was not given the attire to come, or this person was given the attire, but refused to wear it.

Beloved, once you are in Christ, you have been given a white garment to wear. And He expects you to wear it. I struggle with this about as much as anyone. Of all women, I am the least worthy to be found wearing white. When I look back over my life, it is hard for me to believe that I am clean. However, I must be careful when I look back now for it can be very easy for me to slip that white garment off to reveal the stained, smelly clothes underneath. And before I know it, I have slipped back into my old identity. There is a difference in examining who we once were, and in wearing her again. It seems that it is when I am most unsatisfied with my circumstances, that I am most tempted to go back to wearing those old clothes again. Just like this man who was caught red handed at the wedding not properly dressed, God has taken hold of me and said, *"Rhonda, what are you doing here dressed in that?"* And I find myself speechless, just like the man in the parable. It is so easy to forget that we are the **bride**! We were made to wear white! So often I hear Jesus speaking the words of Acts 10: 15 over me, *"What God has made clean, do not call unclean."* Beloved, when we go back to wearing that old self, it is no longer just you that you are setting yourself up against. It is God! And there is no way that we can win against Him.

Remember the words of Ephesians 5:25-27, *"Husbands, love your wives, as Christ loved the church and gave Himself up for her, that he might sanctify her, having cleansed her by the washing of water with the word, so that He might present the church to himself in splendor, without spot or wrinkle and any such thing, that she might be holy and without blemish."* Beloved, we might not always think it matters what we wear out into the world, but it matters very much to our husband, Jesus.

Sometimes, all we can do is the very thing we least feel like doing, sitting at His side, and asking Him to wash the stains away from us with His word. And these are the moments we find that it is the very thing He has been wanting to do most.

Please, take a moment here and pray. Ask Jesus to examine your heart to see if there is anything that He wants to wash away from you right now. And let Him beloved, however long it takes, stay right with Him until you are His spotless bride again.

DAY 5

"For many are called, but few are chosen." (Matthew 22:14)

"The one who conquers will be clothed thus in white garments, and I will never blot out his name out of the book of life. I will confess his name before my Father and before His angels." (Revelation 3:5)

There is a plaque hanging above the doorway of what was once our daughter's nursery. It reads, "we dreamed of you." I bought it while I was pregnant with her. My pregnancy with her was very difficult and I had experienced a miscarriage just before becoming pregnant with Hope. We had a condition called intrauterine growth restriction. Basically, she was not growing as well as she should have due to the inability of my body to supply her with all that she needed to thrive. This is a picture of what it looks like to belong to Christ. In ourselves, we do not have what we need to thrive. We are stuck in a place where we cannot become who it is we need to be to have life. Yet, in our condition, Jesus reaches out to choose us, and give us His own life in order to meet what we are lacking.

There is a perfect display of this in our scripture reading for today.

Meet me in Revelation 3, and let's read verses 1-6 together and then answer the questions that follow.

In verse 1, what is Jesus' observation of the church in Sardis?

____

____

____

____

____

In verses 2-3, what is His prescription for the church?

____

____

____

____

____

In verse 4, what is He describing?

____

____

____

____

In verse 5, what does He say will be given the one who conquers?

____

____

____

____

Considering what you have just read, how do you think one conquers?

____

____

____

____

I love the words from verse 2, *"Wake-up, and strengthen what remains and is about to die, for I have not found your works complete in the sight of my God."* The words remind me of Jesus' last moments before His arrest in the Garden of Gethsemane when He kept asking Peter and John to *stay awake and pray, for the Spirit is willing, but the flesh is weak.* And we know that they just could not resist the urge to sleep.

The words, "Wake up," are profound. Just as we studied earlier this week how we are to pay attention to what God has said, we must first wake-up in order that we might pay attention. This world and all the hustle and bustle associated with it can lull our heart and spirit to sleep so quickly. I mentioned my pregnancy with Hope earlier, because of her condition I had to have weekly ultrasounds to check on her growth. The moment that she began to show signs of not thriving, we were going to have to deliver her. My chances of making it full term were very slim, and we didn't quite make it. She was 5 weeks early. Watching her in the NICU was one of the most heart-breaking times of my life. The first time I saw her, two days after she was born, she was hooked up to so many wires and tubes that I could hardly even touch her. Each wire and tube represented a hurdle that we had to overcome for her to come home.

One of the greatest challenges came at feeding time. She only had a 30-minute window of opportunity to try and eat for her to stand a chance at gaining weight before the burden of eating took more energy than she was gaining from the food. The problem was that, instead of eating, she just wanted to sleep. Tears of frustration would stream down my face as I tried every trick I could think of to coax her into choosing the bottle over sleeping. She was too little to understand the consequences of what her choice would mean. It would mean that she was going to have to stay away from me longer, and it may mean more tubes (physical pain for her, and emotional pain for me). In a matter of moments, she had been taken from my body and my heart was broken that she was now in a place where I could not protect her and sustain her. Jesus showed me so much about His love through that experience. **We were taken from His body, and our white garments are not just about what we wear, they represent our connection in Him**. Like the wires and tubes were a sign of what kept me apart from my little girl, so the stains that we wear represent what keeps us apart from Him. And just as I was frustrated when my daughter chose sleep over fighting to eat so that she could become stronger and come home with me, I often wonder if Jesus experienced frustration when we choose to stay lulled in this world over fighting to eat and allowing Him to keep us in His presence, unstained by the world. **You see, our stains are not just about what we wear, they are about what is wearing us.** Jesus paid such a precious price for our white garments so that He could keep us unstained from the world. Free to live with Him and in Him.

"For many are called, but few are chosen." (Matthew 22:14) Beloved, Jesus has a sign over His heart that reads, "I dreamed of you." Long before you were ever born, you existed in the heart and dreams of Jesus. We must stay awake and aware, so that our lives can conform to His dreams for us. For only His dreams are good and true. Only His dreams conform to the life and eternal purpose that He chose for you long before you were ever born.

Please, close in prayer asking Jesus to help you stay awake and unstained.

Week 6:
Saying Yes to the Dress (Part 2)

DAY 1

"...Come, I will show you the bride, the wife of the Lamb." (Revelation 21:9)

"Therefore, if anyone is in Christ, he is a new creation. The old has passed away; behold the new has come." (2 Corinthians 5:17)

My grandmother recently passed away, leaving me to inherit one of her most treasured possessions, her mother's wedding dress. Her mother made the dress by hand; it took almost a year to make it. As a little girl, I marveled at it and wondered if I might be able to wear it one day when I grew up and got married. I find myself wondering what my great-grandmother must have thought about as she painstakingly sewed her dress together, piece by piece, making sure that everything was perfect for her big day. I wonder if she ever was tempted to settle for a simpler gown, to not have to subscribe to so much detail. And I often wonder if she thought about her groom while she was making that dress. I imagine that it was her thoughts of him, and the way that she wanted to become so beautiful for him on their big day that kept her on course, stitch by stitch, sewing that beautiful gown until the reality of it matched up with the dream in her mind of how she wanted to appear to him. I am sure that the look in his eyes at his first glance of her was worth every single hour spent sewing that dress together. It is amazing how we can live our whole lives seeking out a moment.

One day, you and I will stand before our groom, Jesus, and be radiant in a gown that we spent our whole lives knitting together, righteous deed by righteous deed, until a wedding garment fit perfectly for the bride of Christ becomes complete. We will stand before our Groom and the look in His eyes at that moment will be completely worth it.

I know there are many reading this who have not experienced being a bride in this world. Maybe you even fear that you will never know what it feels like to be a bride on her wedding day. Beloved, rest assured, you are a bride and there is a time coming when you will get to experience the glorious wonder of what it is to be a bride on her wedding day.

One thing we can know for sure about what our attire on that day is that it will be the most radiant sight in our Beloved Bridegroom's eyes, all decked out in a gown that this world is not worthy of, a gown of pure , radiant white!

Meet me in Revelation 19:6-9 and let's take a closer look at this scene.

In verse 7, there is an event that is taking place, what is it?

____

____

____

____

____

Please, fill in the blanks below based on verse 7:

And his bride has _________________ _________________ _________________.

Those words hit me every time. It is easy to sit back and think that it is all up to Jesus to make us ready, and in so many ways, that is true. However, there is some great responsibility to be taken on our part. We will spend our homework this week looking more into what that looks like. We want to be brides who *"make herself ready."*

At the same time, we see another dynamic happening right here in verse 8. Let's look closely at this verse and see how it relates to verse 7.

Fill in the blanks to verse 8 below.

"It was _____________________ her to clothe herself with fine linen, bright and pure— for the fine linen is the ____ of the saints."

To better understand the significance of the fine linen, we must remember that linen was the prescribed material for the priests to wear, it was also what the kittel was made from (the wedding garment), as well as the type of cloth used for burial.

However, what is most important about this verse is not the linen itself, it is the word, "granted."

In your own words, define the word "granted "below.

____

____

____

____

____

Merriam-Webster defines the word "grant" as: *to agree to give, or allow, to give, legally or formally.*

As we truly consider how Revelation 21:7-8 applies to us today, we must keep in mind that we do have a responsibility to *"make ourselves ready"* for our wedding day with Christ. However, in order to do so, we must accept what has been granted to us which is His righteousness.

In your own words, describe what your responsibility is in "making yourself ready" for the marriage supper of the Lamb.

____

____

____

____

____

"Therefore, if anyone is in Christ, he is a new creation. The old has passed away; behold the new has come." (2 Corinthians 5:17)

The words above take on new life to us as we consider how they relate to our lives here in Christ. Beloved, the moment you trusted Him and asked Him into your heart, you literally became a whole new creation in Him. Everything about your old life passed away. You may have not completely understood it, and probably won't understand it fully until we get to be with Him in glory. You probably, like me, had no idea how to live like this was true about you. However, it does not change the fact that this is true about you. You are a new creation, Beloved, each day, Jesus has laid out your clothes for you. He has granted you permission to wear His righteousness into the world. **It is not something you have to do; it is who you have now become in Christ.** When you put Him on, and walk out of the door each day, you don't have to try and be righteous. You already are, you simply allow yourself to conform to the new creation that through His grace, He has allowed you to become.

He has granted, and all we must do is receive His righteousness, and wear who He is in our lives.

There is a perfect story in the Bible of how this relates to our lives and we will spend much of our week learning from the woman with the issue of blood. She represents all of us who Jesus has allowed to become someone more than she ever thought possible simply by receiving His righteousness.

Let's close in prayer thanking Jesus for allowing us to be granted His righteousness and also for allowing us to know and learn more about what it looks like to wear Him in this world.

DAY 2

"Therefore, if anyone is in Christ, he is a new creation. The old has passed away; behold the new has come." (2 Corinthians 5:17)

"He is clothed in a robe dipped in blood, and the name by which he is called is The Word of God," (Revelation 19:13)

We briefly talked about what happens once the bride enters the wedding destination after she and the groom are carried all the way back to the father's house for the second part of the wedding to take place. The bride and groom are prepared, and both enter the bridal chamber where they will remain for the next seven days. The bride is veiled as she enters, a sign that she has kept herself for her husband and is ready to be unveiled for him alone. The first order of business upon entry into the bridal chamber is the consummation of the wedding. The bride and groom make love while the guests are outside awaiting the glorious news that the covenant between them is officially consummated. The news was often delivered through the groom holding out the white sheet with blood on it, the blood symbolized that the wife had kept her purity and had now given herself fully to her husband.

Just as in our wedding to Christ, the blood ensures our purity and shows us visibly how our beloved Jesus has given Himself fully to us and for us. We, as His Bride, had no purity to offer, so He provided both, our purity, and the blood to display our purity.

We can even see this depiction in scripture, meet me in Revelation 19:11-14 and let's read these verses together and answer the questions that follow.

In verse 13 what does it say that Jesus is wearing?

____

____

____

____

And what is His name in that same verse?

____

____

____

____

In verse 14, what does it say that we are wearing?

____

____

____

____

You may be thinking, I thought that it was the bride's blood that was displayed on the wedding day. Well, in all truth it is our blood. Hebrews 12:12 says, *"So Jesus also suffered outside the gate in order to sanctify the people through His own blood."* Also in Luke 22:20, He says," *And likewise the cup after they had eaten, saying, "This cup that is poured out for you is the new covenant of my blood."*

We are not a pure bride in and of ourselves; therefore, we have no blood to offer on our wedding day. Romans 3: 10-12 assures us that, *"none is righteous, no, not one; no one understands; no one understands; no one seeks God. All have turned aside; together they have become worthless; no one does good, not even one."*

When Jesus appears to the world, with us riding behind Him, the blood He is wearing is to display our righteousness, a righteousness that He paid dearly for. Just as a true Hebrew groom does in fulfilling the contents of his ketubah, even if it means paying for the sins of his bride with his life, our beloved Jesus kept His promise to us, giving up His own spotless blood for the redemption of His Bride, us, His Church.

As I mentioned yesterday, there is a beautiful depiction of this in the gospel of Luke 40-48. Meet me there as we look at one example of a woman who was unclean becoming clean through an encounter with Jesus. In one brief encounter, she not only lost her old identity as a woman who was unclean, but she was also given a new identity, an identity as a daughter of God.

So, it is with you and I, beloved. As we relate with her over these next couple of days, let's not forget that we, just like her, have been given the unimaginable privilege of exchanging our unclean identity in this world for that of a righteous daughter of God.

In fact, let's take a moment right now to affirm this truth. Please, fill in your name in the blank below.

I, ____, am the daughter of God!

In fact, let's double affirm this truth. Write your name also in the blanks below.

"Therefore, if _________________ is in Christ, (s)he is a new creation. The old _________________ has passed away; behold the new _________________ has come." 2 Corinthians 5:17 (emphasis mine)

As you reflect on the two statements above, do you feel as if they are true about you?

____

____

____

____

____

If so, how? If not, why?

____

____

____

____

____

Beloved, regardless of how you feel. You **are** a new creation in Christ if you have ever truly reached out for Him and asked Him to make what happened at the Cross count for you. If you are uncertain in any way, why not take a moment right now and reach out for Him, just as this woman did who had the issue of blood. Not much different from any of us, she simply knew she was at the end of herself and was desperate enough to reach out for Jesus. And just as He did for her, so He will also do for you, *"Daughter, your faith has made you well; go now in peace."*

Let's close in prayer either asking Jesus to come into our hearts and to give us His life changing blood, or just spend these moments thanking Him for the moment when He touched us and made us new through the power of His blood.

____

____

____

____

DAY 3

"And whoever touches the body of the one with the discharge shall wash his clothes, and bath himself with water and be unclean until evening," (Leviticus 15:7)

"And there was a woman who had had a discharge of blood for twelve years, and though she had spent all of her living on physicians, she could not be healed by anyone." (Luke 8:43)

We briefly met this woman yesterday. She is known forever in scripture as the woman with the issue of blood. I love that she remains nameless, for there have been so many times in my own life where I, like her, have reached out for the hem of Christ's garment and in so doing immersed myself in her identity. She was a woman who was completely bankrupt in every sense of the word; financially, emotionally, socially, and physically. How often we refuse to come to Jesus until we find ourselves in her shoes. Hopeless and bankrupt, we become fully aware that we have run out of options for hope in any other direction. It is then that we often look up and allow our hope to extend to the One who is outside of us. And so often, we come to Him from behind, almost sneaking up, hoping no one will notice, that no one will ask anything of us. For the first time in our lives, we realize that we have nothing, *absolutely nothing* to offer. **Reaching beyond ourselves, we reach out to Him and our hope explodes as we sense a filling, a healing filling unlike any we have ever experienced in this life**. For so many of us, it is the first time we truly experience what *real love* is, for He is *real love*. And as much as we know we don't deserve Him, we can't help but take what He is offering to us. If only we could stay in this moment forever, it would be enough. **This is the moment every other moment in our lives seems to have been leading up to.**

Do you know what I mean? Have you experienced this moment with Jesus? If so, please, share below.

____

____

____

____

If not, let's spend some time with the women who has, and let's share in her experience in hopes that we too might come to know Jesus in a new way, that He might reveal Himself once more to us as we press in to know Him more. Beloved, I know that He is waiting for you to know Him more.

Meet me once more in Luke 8 and let's begin by reading verses 40-42 together and answering the questions below.

In verse 40, the situation that Jesus and this woman were in is described, write below how you picture the scene.

____

____

____

____

In verse 41, we see a new situation arise, what happens that seems to shift Jesus in a new direction?

____

____

____

____

In verse 42, we learn more about this situation. Describe below what this scene looks like now. Also, think about the people, what are some of the reasons you feel people might have come to see Jesus?

____

____

____

____

____

In verse 42, how old is the little girl? And what was her condition?

____

____

____

____

____

I can imagine that, by this time, word had gotten around about Jesus. He had not only performed amazing miracles in healing, but also taught about God in a way that no one ever experienced before. And perhaps, most scandalous about Him was His reach extended not only to those who were the spiritually elite, but He ministered to all people, even those who were unclean, broken, outcast, and sinners. **Before Jesus, no man had ever witnessed or experienced the scandal of God's grace, but through Him, they were encountering it full on.** And then, just as now, their response to it determined how they truly saw God.

I can imagine that, as news spread that He was making his way towards Jairus' house to heal his daughter, some of the people who came to see a sign, or a miracle become excited. They were going to get to see Jesus in action! Others who may have come to be healed, or to assess for themselves if he might be God or not may have been disappointed that their hopes for access to Jesus were now dashed. Surely, they did not stand a chance when Jairus, the ruler of the synagogue, needed His assistance. And He was going to heal a little girl, a pure little girl who was dying. Surely anything that they had hoped to experience with Jesus was less important than this.

Verse 43 gives us insight into one person who was in the crowd, the crowd who was now pushing and shoving their way with Jesus as He turned to go heal Jairus' daughter.

What does this verse say about the woman? What is her condition and how long has she had it?

____

____

____

____

____

This woman had an issue of blood, which rendered her unclean in the eyes of her people. Let's look up Leviticus 15:1-12 together and discover the laws that applied to this woman.

Write your impression of what it must have been like live in this woman's shoes below.

____

____

____

____

____

I imagine she was disappointed when Jesus set his attention elsewhere. She was sick, bankrupt, and just about desperate enough to risk anything in order to be healed. He had been her last hope, and now that hope was dashing away to go heal someone much more important than her. I imagine that she began feeling a little down on herself for her disappointment; after all, He was going to heal a little girl, a little girl who was dying, a daughter of a holy one. She was a nobody. Her condition had rendered her unclean and inaccessible to family and social life twelve years earlier. The sickness she experienced and the pain she endured from it paled in comparison to the loneliness the condition left her in. She had been unclean for so many years that she did not even hope for the comfort of human relationships anymore. Doctor after doctor had taken her money and her hope with promises of healing and restoration. Now she had nothing, nothing but to wait out her life of rejection, loneliness, and the pain.

Have you ever been there sweet one? Finally taken that step that represented such risk in your life, and yet when you got there, your hope was dashed? Write about it here.

____

____

____

____

____

What about this, have you ever felt like other people are more deserving of Jesus' healing or attention than you are? Why? What was that like for you? Please, share below.

____

____

____

____

____

Beloved, with Jesus there is always another side to the story. It may look like He is moving mountains for someone else while you are still in that same "unclean" spot. Perhaps, like this woman, you have finally risked exposing yourself to Him, or risked greater faith in Him through stepping out in an earthly relationship (a new friendship, or Bible study group, job, or even romantic relationship). You have tried to walk with Jesus to a new place. You are reaching out for Him in a way that requires great risk, and it seems that He has turned His face in another direction. May I encourage you to keep reaching sweet one? Reaching for Jesus is always a good idea, and no matter what your prior life experiences have been, He **never** disappoints. That distance between where you are and where He is requires faith, and we are assured in Romans 10:11, "*Whoever believes in Him will not be disappointed.*"

Let's close in prayer, thanking God for a new hope and courage to keep reaching for Jesus, no matter what.

DAY 4

"But Jesus said, 'Someone touched me, for I perceive that power has gone out from me.'" (Luke 8:46)

Let's pick up right where we left off yesterday in looking at the woman with the issue of blood. About now, you may be wondering if I forgot that this is a Bible study about how we are Christ's beloved bride. Well, I have not forgotten. And just to prove it, I am going to share with you how this relates. If you can remember, after the bride and groom enter the bridal chamber, their first act as husband and wife is to consummate the marriage vows. She is to press her body into his, while he is doing the same into hers. Sorry, I know this is a little graphic, but we are all adults, right? So, there is vulnerability involved, there is pressing, and there is blood. So, as you can see, in observing this woman, we have our perfect candidate for showing us a little lesson on what it is to truly consummate our marriage with Christ. The precious truth for us is that, when we allow ourselves to press into Him, the automatic response from Him is Life. Well, I am getting a little ahead of myself. Let's get back to where we left off.

We left off talking about Luke 8:40- 43, and we were talking about how this unclean woman had ended up in the last place she was supposed to be, a crowd of people following Jesus. The following is just my idea of how things might have gone.

The last glimmer of hope had surfaced in her heart when she overheard some people talking about how Jesus healed a beggar, a nobody just like her. She also heard other stories about how Jesus talked to tax collectors, and taught about how people who are hungry, and poor like her are blessed. She wanted to know more about all of this. It just seemed too good to be true. Had God really come to them, and if so, could He really love or even care about her? She had to know. But wanting this knowledge would mean placing herself at great risk. She knew there were others like her, who wanted to know more about Jesus. She knew that to expose herself to Him meant exposing herself to everyone else. Because she was unclean, this was breaking the law, and not only would she risk her life in the process, but she would also risk the lives of those whom she touched. Had she really stooped that low? Was she so desperate to get to Jesus that she was willing to hurt others by making them unclean in the process?

For twelve years she carried the weight of knowing she was a threat to any person who encountered her, the weight that was now nearly burying her. And now, despite herself, her feet were headed straight for the crowd of people, all gathering in on her as they followed Jesus. Her heart pounded as the weight of twelve years of rule following began lifting from her, even as those around pressed in even more. She had the choice to yell out, "unclean" and admit the truth about herself, while also admitting that she was choosing to expose all those around her in the crowd to her uncleanness as well. Or she could just duck out and get out of there as fast as possible, but she had come so far, too far to turn back now, and He had been her only hope. She was close enough now to see the edge of His robe. A mixture of desperation and faith burst through her as she gathered up her last ounce of courage and reached for Him.

Verses 44-48 tell us about the dramatic scene that takes place next. Please, read the verses and answer the questions that follow.

In verse 44, what does it say she touched? And what happened as soon as she did?

____

____

____

____

____

Different translations use the word, "hem" but the most literal translation used the word, "fringe" to talk about what part of Jesus' garment the woman touched. Numbers 15:37-41 tells us about what the "fringe" or tassels on Jesus' garment represents. *Look up these scriptures and write about the purpose of these very special part of Christ's robe.*

____

____

____

____

____

Those little fringes at the end of His robe represented the very purpose for which Christ came, to fulfill the law and become holy so that He could then become the only sacrifice for our sin. Although I am sure she didn't know it and surely, she didn't understand it, but through her one act, she received the gift that Jesus came to give; and that gift is a redeemed life.

What about you? What were you reaching for the very first time that you reached for Jesus? Did you have any idea that He truly was or how much He truly loves you?

____

____

____

____

____

Maybe you were like me, and like this woman, had" *spent all your living"* on what did not satisfy your needs. And so, sheepishly, you reached out for One that you knew you did not understand, in hopes that He might give you the one thing that always seemed unattainable, true love and acceptance.

Do you remember the first time you reached for Him? Can you go back there and share what it was you were hoping He might satisfy in your life?

____

____

____

____

____

Jesus is so amazing; His love for us is so great. We come to Him for our own reasons, and have no idea at the time, that He will eventually make us His own, that He will become our one reason and our one hope. Just as this woman reached out for Him in her time of greatest desperation, may we never stop reaching for Him throughout our lives. Even our reaching for Him is generated from Him, He teaches us to need Him and then becomes the One we need.

Verse 45-46 fills us in on what happens when she (and we) reach out to touch Him.

———————————————————————————————————

———————————————————————————————————

———————————————————————————————————

———————————————————————————————————

———————————————————————————————————

"Who touched me?" these words must have thundered in her heart like an earthquake. Her moment of greatest triumph had just turned into her moment of greatest humiliation. Not only had she touched the One who was Holy, but also now she was exposed to everyone. Every person there would know the truth about her, that she had been unclean, and had not only exposed Him to her uncleanness, but each one of them too.

Verse 47 tells about her moment of spilling the beans. The verse characterizes her as trembling and falling before His feet. I can only imagine that she felt her life was over at this point. I can't help but think of the words from John 8:32 at this moment, *"you shall know the truth, and the truth shall set you free."* So often we want to push into Jesus for our own personal reasons. **We sneak into church, we skim through relationships, staying hidden all the time, never really trying to know or expose ourselves to anyone**. But, once we know Jesus, we realize quickly that He does not let us get away with ourselves. He is always after one thing, and that is **our truth**. He always wants our truth because He just can't wait to exchange it for **His truth** about us. Just when this woman thought her life was over, *it was.* Her life as an unclean woman was over. Jesus would not let her off the hook with just a healing; He was after *her complete restoration.*

In Hebrew culture, one cannot simply be healed and re-enter society. For her to be accepted back into normal relationships, she had to be presented as clean publicly. What looked to this woman to be Jesus confronting her publicly was actually Him restoring her publicly. He was bringing her back into right relationship not only with Himself, but also with everyone who once perceived her as unclean. Had He not afforded her this opportunity, even though she had been healed, she might have lived out the rest of her life as unclean.

This may seem like an odd concept, however as one who has walked through a very long season of sickness, I can relate. There came a time when I noticed that I was moving more towards healing than towards my life ending here on earth. I want to be very sensitive here because I realize that not everyone is afforded that opportunity.

I can't fully understand why it was granted to me. There were about four years when I was unsure whether more time was an option for me, and you live your life from a different set of lenses when you are living in total awareness that life on earth may be winding down for you. I consider those years as a great gift, a glimpse of what it is to live so sensitive and aware of each moment before the face of Jesus. There came a time when Jesus asked me to publicly announce that I was headed back to where I had left off before my health crisis began. I did it in my Bible study, a room full of women I know, love and trust. It was a very important moment for me. A moment where I was able to declare before God and others that I am receiving the season that Jesus ordained for me. To be honest, it wasn't easy. There is a sense of surrender you enter when you are a Christian that is very ill for a long time. It's a beautiful place where you settle into the *whatever of God*. It's humbling to admit that I wasn't there before that season, but there are just some doors that only the key of suffering can unlock.

And once you are there, you know the next step is heaven – home. And in some weird way, there is peace and I dare say even a joy that comes once you are finally re-solved to that.

It took a while for me to realize that Jesus was asking me to hand Him back the key, leave that room, and get back to where I left off before that whole journey began.

It feels kind of like entering back into the wrestling match to try and win something you already won. It's hard to hand back the key to a door He allowed you to unlock.

With Jesus, it's all about faith. It took faith for me to enter the rest that all would be well should He take me home. And now it takes faith for me to believe that I can be well, and stay in His rest, even after a long season of illness, even as I trade in my sick girl lenses for made-well girl ones. I have learned and am still learning to see myself as He sees me, nothing more, yet nothing less. **And sometimes that means agreeing with Him when He has graced me with a new season, even if I don't understand it or feel I deserve it.** I receive it because the One Who made me said so. I believe Jesus wants us to always experience the glory of who He has caused us to become, no matter what season it is He is calling us to walk through with Him. **We are prone to get stuck in old identities tied to old seasons.** I could feel myself becoming a patient and could have easily succumbed to that identity and kept one foot in a hospital sock, with the other out in the world. But it was time to believe that He was leading me out of that season and I needed to experience myself as His new creation, a daughter who He had redeemed from death to life, to walk with Him, and trust Him, no matter what.

This makes me wonder about you. Is there an area in your life where you have allowed Jesus to heal you, maybe you have even allowed Him to confront you? Perhaps, you might even be struggling with resenting Him a bit because He seems to be confronting you. Maybe, like this woman He is asking you to make something public to those around you that you just don't feel comfortable doing. Or maybe, He is asking you to enter a new realm of relationship with people that are complete strangers to you through service, or a career move. Or, like me, maybe He as asking you to close the door on a chapter of your life that was very personal and took a lot of courage for you to walk through-and it's hard because you aren't sure who you are on the other side of it. But He's calling you to experience yourself in a new way. I don't know what it is, but I know He is not going to give up on you. He is after your complete freedom, and He will not let you go until you are fully redeemed.

Let's close in prayer thanking Him for His never ending, never giving up kind of love.

DAY 5

"And he said to her, 'Daughter, your faith has made you well, go in peace.' (Luke 8:48)

"Blessed are those who wash their robes, so that they may have the right to the tree of life and that they may enter the city by the gate." (Revelation 22:14)

We have come to almost the end of our journey with the woman who had the issue of blood. And I don't know about you, but I have learned so much through her. One thing that I forgot to mention yesterday was the word used for power in verse 46, where it says, *"But Jesus said, "Someone touched me, for I perceive that power has gone out from me."* The Greek word for power is *dunamis*; it means not only power, but also miraculous power, violent power, abundant power or abundant force. We must remember that at the time of her healing, there were many people pressing into Jesus. So, we can know that the pressing taking place in her case was different from mere physical contact or proximity. We can gather from Jesus' words to her in verse 48 that she has an extra ingredient in her pressing that made all the difference.

In the space below, re-write the words from the verse 48 below.

Faith! It is the miracle-producing ingredient. We can press into Jesus all day long, but until we press into Him with faith, nothing will happen. However, when we do add faith into our pressing, we can expect a wonderful outcome, a *dunamis* outcome! We can gather from this story that the response from Jesus' release of power was automatic. His power responds to faith, and once faith is pressed into Him, His power can't help but be released.

Let's take a moment and look up a few verses about faith. Look up the following verse and record what they say about faith.

Matthew 17:20

____

____

____

____

Romans 3:28

____

____

____

____

Romans 10:17

____

____

____

____

Hebrews 11:1

____

____

____

____

Hebrews 11:6

____

____

____

____

Faith in Christ is what allows Him to invite us to know Him in the beginning, and our faith is the gasoline that will fuel us towards Him all the way to the end. Just as we heard His words over us in the beginning, *"daughter, your faith has made you well, go in peace,"* so we will hear those words over us all throughout our lives with Christ. For once we become well in one area in our lives, there is another one to conquer. So, our whole lives are lived out as one great big journey in seeing Jesus redeem us again and again. It's our sanctification journey, our long walk down the wedding aisle with Him. **Each step, leaving us with another piece of our own redeemed heart, to have and to hold, from that day forward**. Until one day we enter glory, and hear these words, *"Blessed are those who wash their robes, so that they may have the right to the tree of life and that they may enter the city by the gate." (Revelation 22:14).* Each and every time Jesus reaches down to wash us here on earth, He is fulfilling His husbandly duties as prescribed in Eph. 5:26, *"that he might sanctify (remember that the Hebrew word for marry is sanctify) her, having cleansed her with the washing of water with the word."* His job is to continually wash us and sanctify us our whole lives until we appear with Him in glory. And our job is to let Him. Just as we would allow ourselves to live, move, and breath in a human marriage relationship, so we are in our heavenly one. Right now, in heaven, there is no greater business on Jesus' agenda than watching over His bride. You are simply the apple of His eye. It seems too easy to believe that all we must do to be

His is to be on the receiving end of this agreement, but that is exactly what is true about this marriage relationship.

If you don't believe me, look up the following two verses, which talk about what will happen to those who are not on the receiving end of the relationship.

After looking up the following two verses, record what they have in common below.

Revelation 20:12; 22:12.

At the end of our lives, we will either answer for our actions or for all Jesus accomplished on our behalf. It is our choice here that confirms what eternal experience it will be. As His bride, He takes complete responsibility for our lives here, with the result being that we can dwell with Him eternally in heaven. He is the perfect Husband who has fulfilled and is continually fulfilling His ketubah agreement with each one of us who humbly let Him. He is the initiator as well as the keeper of our marriage to Him. Our part is to realize by faith who we are. And when we choose to walk away from our ketubah covenant agreement (which we all do at times), His mercy and grace covers all our sin, all our mistakes. Just as the He stated at the Sermon on the Mount, *"blessed are you when you are poor, for yours is the kingdom of God."* Just like the woman with the issue of blood, all that is required of us is to show Jesus the truth about us, and He is there ready to wash our truth away and replace it with His. *"Blessed are those who wash their robes, so that they may have the right to the tree of life and that they may enter the city by the gate."* (Revelation 22:14)

Let's close this week's lesson in prayer, thanking Him for the faithful husband He is to us all.

Week 7:
The Covering

DAY 1

"After these days his wife Elizabeth conceived, and for five months she kept herself hidden, saying, 'Thus the LORD has done for me in the days when he looked on me, to take away my reproach among people,'" (Luke 1:24-25)

"In the sixth month the angel Gabriel was sent from God to the city of Galilee named Nazareth, to a virgin betrothed to a man whose name was Joseph, of the house of David. And the virgin's name was Mary." (Luke 1:26-27)

There are moments in our Christian journey when the ancient paths that so many before us have taken become our own. There are moments when our feet may still be touching earth, yet we sense a strength moving them forward as coming from a power so much greater than us and know it's this same power that held all that have gone before us. Each one of us is a sojourner, individually discovering the same ancient path that carries us along the blood worn path of our Savior. Some of our most difficult paths become intertwined with an awareness that we are, perhaps, traversing upon the same sacred ground that held up Moses as he beheld that burning bush, Elijah as he stood on the mountain and watched the wind and fire pass by, and Mary who knelt down in the presence of God's glory as an angel explained to her that she had been chosen to carry God's most precious gift to all mankind. The journey is forward, yet we find that we are suddenly propelled by a power that is not our own. We are cloaked in God's covering, and it somehow keeps our feet moving forward throughout our journey here.

As we embark on this final leg of our journey, it is easy to become overwhelmed at how many loose ends there are still left to tie. Yet, there is also a beautiful **freedom** in knowing that is what the Covering is all about. We get to walk into the **rest** of our journey **free** to not know, because we are **covered** by the One Who does.

We will spend our last moments together with two women who Jesus first chose to carve out an ancient path through, a covering that we are still invited to follow today. One of these women is Mary, the mother of Jesus and the other is Mary Magdalene, one of His most trusted and devoted followers.

We will begin by reading the account of Mary, mother of our Lord, we will begin with her cousins, Zechariah and Elizabeth. God's perfect plan always moves in His perfect timing and as we know from our prior study, the friend of the bridegroom always appears before the bridegroom comes.

Meet me in Luke 1 as we behold the miracle and wonder of what God was doing.

Let's read chapter 1 verses 5-56 together as we take in the wonder of how God chose to use the covering of a young girl to one day ensure the covering of us all.

Meet me back here when you are finished so we can linger in the wonder a little longer.

We already know the reason why God is sending John to be born, but as we consider the concept of "covering", how might God's miracle for Zechariah and Elizabeth represent a type of "covering" for Mary? Explain.

____

____

____

____

____

Has God ever sent anything ahead of you (a person or a circumstance) to prepare you for what He was about to do through you? Please, share.

____

____

____

____

____

We've all stepped into a moment that made every other moment feel like they were only the preparation for **this moment**. That is exactly what it must have been like for Zechariah and Elizabeth. In those days, a priest, such as Zechariah, might never be chosen to serve alone in the presence of God in this way (offering incense). This was a moment that he had surely hoped and prayed would someday come. At the same time, there was another moment that he and his wife had been longing for, the hope of being blessed with a child.

In those days, to not be blessed with a child was seen to be as having been cursed by God. Yet verse 6 assures us that both Zechariah and Elizabeth walked blamelessly before God.

Isn't just like our Lord to ask us to come anyway, and stand before Him, even with the gaping questions in our souls left unanswered, as we watch Him become our answer to them all?

Zechariah was sent to offer up incense, representing the prayers of the people rising before God. I love the thought of our prayers rising before Him, even now, in the form of a smoky fragrance. What to us looks like a heavy fog of frustration, often presented in a mixture of tears and fear over the fog of a future life we simply cannot see, arises to God in the form of a fragrant offering, pleasing all the more because in them lies the sacrifice of a heart that is willing to let them go. That is really all He wants, our hearts released to His, no matter how foggy and confusing they seem. In His Presence, they become a pleasing aroma.

It's a blessing to know our Father is always pleased to receive our authentic hearts.

We find in this scared moment between God and Zechariah, the priest serving Him, our first look at the concept of covering.

If you remember from our study, the wedding term that bears the meaning for covering is Huppah. It is the place where the bridegroom and the bride will first meet to consummate their marriage vows. They will then stay in the Huppah for seven days as they continue to become acquainted with one another as their hearts have longed to do during the whole waiting process.

A mixture of smoke and glory ushered in a whole new view of God than Zechariah (or anyone else for that matter) had experienced up to that point. The God Whom he had prayed to and believed in suddenly became the One who answered back, and not only that, the One who was calling Zechariah and his wife to become part of His story.

Based on Zechariah's response, do you think he believed God was going to do what He said He would?

____

____

____

____

____

How did the angel respond to Zechariah's response to what God had said?

____

____

____

____

____

I find it fascinating that the angel took Zachariah's voice away. I cannot imagine how frustrating this must have been, yet as I think about it now, I can see that it may have been God's mercy that caused Him to respond in such a way.

Sometimes, we use our words to uncover what God is trying to cover us in.

I believe that God saw a propensity in Zechariah for this to happen and decided it might just be best to leave him sitting in what God alone had to say rather than risk him trying to add to it with his own powerless words.

It takes a mighty strong person to trust that what God has said is enough, and to let those words be all the covering that is needed. It takes some of us a lifetime to become such a person.

What about you? Have you ever talked yourself out of God's covering? If so, how? Why?

____

____

____

____

____

Why not take a moment here to give Him the chance to let you come back under His covering and find the rest He longs to give you. Take a moment here and pray.

____

____

____

____

____

We will look at a few observations before linking it in relation to Mary's story. First, let's look at Elizabeth in verses 24-25 and answer the questions below.

Did Elizabeth conceive? Yes or no?

____

____

____

____

____

Sounds silly, but just wanted to take a moment and remind us all that God does what **He says He will do**. He is faithful!

How long did Elizabeth stay hidden?

____

____

____

____

____

Elizabeth, who many may have seen as cursed by God, or even stricken with disease for her inability to conceive, did not go out and announce to the world that she was pregnant, and that God released her from her time of waiting.

What an amazing woman!

Instead, she chose to enter, along with her husband, the quiet wonder of God's grace.

Her time of waiting for God to move was over, and now she was able to take full advantage of waiting in the stillness and beauty of watching what happens when one has taken her covering under the shelter of her King.

Can you image watching your belly that you must have looked at a million times and believed to be cursed and barren, suddenly rise, all because God told it to?

What a MIRACLE!

The number five in the bible corresponds with God's grace.

God was coming to open a door through the wombs of two women, one who would carry the friend of the Bridegroom, and one who would carry the Bridegroom Himself.

"Oh, the depth of the riches of the wisdom and knowledge of God! How unsearchable his judgements, and his paths beyond tracing out." Romans 11:33

Sometimes, God does something SO big that there are no words!

Grace is one of those things. We can't describe it, we can only watch it rise out of a dead place in us and then run out into the all the world and show them the Life that God, Himself, has become in us.

I want to close today with our first look at Mary, meet me in Luke 1 as we read verses 26-27 together.

Jot down anything that stands out to you below.

____

____

____

____

____

A new covering is taking place, our heavenly One.

The number six corresponds with man in the bible.

God was sending the Son of Man to become our Covering. The world would never be the same.

"And the angel answered her, "The Holy Spirit will come upon you, and the power of the Most High will overshadow you; therefore the child to be born will be called holy-"the Son of God." (Luke 1:35)

DAY 2

"And the angel answered her, 'The Holy Spirit will come upon you, and the power of the Most High will overshadow you; therefore the child to be born will be called holy,-the Son of God.'" (Luke 1:35)

"For God so loved the world that He gave His only begotten Son, that whoever believes in Him should not perish but have everlasting life." (John 3:16)

We left off yesterday with an angel on the way to make the announcement that would change all our lives. Let's pick up there and read Luke 1:26-38, before meeting me back here.

My heart leaps with joy for Mary, and for all of us, who, like her, have found it difficult to comprehend just why God would choose her. Verse 29 depicts this beautifully as it says, *"But she was greatly troubled at this saying, and tried to discern what sort of greeting this might be."* The NKJV states it this way: *"But when she saw him, she was troubled at his saying, and considered what manner of greeting this was."*

To understand the reason for Mary's worry we must *consider* her surroundings. Of all the places one could live at that time, Nazareth was the least. To live in Nazareth was the polar opposite of being *"favored."* When I drive through certain areas of town, I lock my doors because I don't sense God's *favor* upon that area. This was Nazareth. It was not a place someone would plan to belong, except for God.

Just to give some back reference on what we are talking about here, let's look at Isaiah 53:1-3 as we consider where Mary and Jesus were from.

Nazareth comes from a Hebrew word meaning *netzar,* which means, *"branch"* or *"shoot."* Sometimes when a tree is chopped down, a shoot will grow from the stump, allowing a new tree to spring up from where the old one has died. That shoot is called, *netzar.*

As we consider these verses from Isaiah 53 that prophesy about the coming of our Lord, we are filled with new wonder that He would literally be born to a mother from Nazareth. Our Root, Jesus, would spring up from the driest of ground, ensuring a safe covering for each of us who have felt despised and rejected in this world.

What is it like to know that God came to Nazareth to implant Jesus?

____

____

____

____

____

There was nothing about Mary that deserved the gift God was bringing, except that she had the kind of heart that was "implantable." What beautiful freedom comes when we consider that all God really wants from us is to allow Him to implant the wonder of His Son in us.

I want us to *consider* Mary's response to this encounter. We get really confused when we approach scripture mindlessly and, though we will never fully understand all there is to know until we enter heaven, we are encouraged to, "*...lay hold of that for which Christ Jesus has also laid hold of me.*" *(Philippians 3:12)*

Sometimes our "*knower*" can get in the way of knowing Christ, but I love how Mary displays a mixture of both reverence and wisdom in her response to God's choosing her.

The word *considered* that we find in verse 29 in Greek is *dialogizomai.* It stems from the word; *dia,* which means an intensive and *logizomai,* which means to reckon through, to settle accounts.

I don't know about you, but this just blesses my heart and brings me to tears. It's just so God! Here is an angel showing up to the least likely girl in the least likely town, calling her the least likely name, "*favored one*," and her mind is reeling as she tries to *settle the accounts* for how this can be?

Have you ever been there, beloved? I know I have. When I get stuck in the *dryness* and *rottenness* of me, and I begin to think it's who I am, Jesus shows up like a stream bursting right through the dry desert of me proclaiming, *"Rejoice, highly favored one..."*

And my every attempt to *settle my account with Him* is met by own awareness that He has already **paid in full** any account I can or will ever bring before Him. He is, and always will be my Covering, my faithful Huppah…all the way home.

How about you? Do you find yourself trying to settle accounts with Jesus? How?

____

____

____

____

____

I can hardly wait to share the next part with you, for it marks the very first time Mary gets to behold her new covering. And I pray we find a new revelation of our covering in this moment as well.

Just after Mary's moment of striving to settle accounts has taken place, what does the angel say to her in verse 30? Please write it below, and as you do, let Jesus spread those precious words over you as well.

____

____

____

____

____

The word, favor, that the angel assures Mary that God has found with her is ***charis*** in Greek. You may recognize that word as it means; grace, the divine influence upon the heart. It not only *is* the influence, but also means how the influence reflects in the life of its recipient, perhaps in the form of joy, favor, and thanks.

Grace, the substance of all our Covering first began in a moment when a young, frightened girl looked into the face of an angel who told her she was more than she knew, and as she searched for a way to reconcile the irreconcilable, God reached down from heaven to unlock a knowing in her heart that overcame the knowing she held in her head. **Grace comes when we become aware that we cannot pay, and in an instant, we take shelter in the Only One Who can, that's Jesus, our Covering.**

"He brought me to the banquet hall, and his banner over me is love." (Song of Solomon 2:4, ISV)

We usually look at the incarnation and make Mary the center of the story, but I want to spend the rest of our time today placing all glory and honor on the only One to Whom it is due.

Based on the definition of favor, what was Mary's part in the birth story?

____

____

____

____

____

Verses 31-38 give us more details on the actualization of God's plan.

How does Mary respond to the instructions the angel is giving her in verses 34-35? And how does this differ from her cousin, Zachariah's response to the news that he will be entrusted with a miracle birth?

____

____

____

____

____

We don't know for certain. On the outside, it looks like their responses are almost the same, two people asking God, *"how will this happen?"*

But, based on the angel's response to Zachariah and the angel's response to Mary, we can see that one responded in disbelief to what God was saying, and the other with a believing heart. We can *act* like we believe God all we want, but He sees our hearts and I find it very convicting to see evidence of that right here.

As we go forward considering God's part in the birth story, we will spend the remainder of our time contemplating the wonder of these two verses.

"And the angel answered her, "The Holy Spirit will come upon you, and the power of the Most High will overshadow you; therefore the child to be born will be called holy 'the Son of God.'" (Luke 1:35)

"*For God so loved the world that He gave His only begotten Son, that whoever believes in Him should not perish but have everlasting life." (John 3:16)*

I don't know any other scripture that portrays the idea of covering as well as Luke 1:35 does. I have such a vivid imagination and I have often wondered what it was like for Mary when the *"…Most High overshadowed her."* Did she know it? Was it terrifying and wonderful all at the same time?

My research has led me to believe that the moment happened almost immediately after this encounter with the angel, perhaps even during this encounter. Scripture doesn't give us any more insight other than to inform us that Mary would soon catch the next donkey ride to see her cousin Elizabeth. This leads me to believe that, like us, Mary wanted to see the confirmation of what God has said to her heart.

I love that Mary was like us, a mixture of ordinary and supernatural wonder all at the same time! Carrying the glory of God, yet still needing to see the evidence of what she held inside of her…outside of her.

God knows there are times we need His covering and grace here on earth, and He graciously grants it. We see this from the very beginning with two women who, entrusted with carrying God's kingdom, still found comfort in seeing the evidence of that kingdom in one another.

Who has God placed in your life to be living proof of His evidence living inside of you? Take a moment to thank Jesus for the hope and joy He brings through them.

John 3:16 is perhaps the world's most well-known scripture, yet there is a beautiful truth tucked inside of it that I often wonder if the world truly understands. It is found inside the words, *only begotten.* Those words, *only begotten,* in Greek are actually one word, **monogenes**. It means, only born, sole, only. The word comes from the root, **mono**, meaning one, and **genos**, meaning kind.

Based on this definition, we see that God was the sole parent of Jesus. Jesus was implanted into Mary, but His DNA was all His Dad's.

This concept is hard to understand, but if we go back to the garden, I think we can find some clarity.

Let's meet at Genesis 1:1, write the scripture here below.

The word for God in this verse is **Elohim**, it means Mighty God! It is a plural noun, meaning one, yet also more than one. It is the name given for God as our Creator. And as we consider this name of God, along with what we know about Him in John 1, we know that Jesus (the Word) was with God in the creation. And that everything that was created was made through Him.

What does John 1 verses 3 and 4 say about Jesus?

____

____

____

____

____

Now, let's go back to the beginning and consider something, let's read Genesis 2:15-17. What did God say would happen if Adam ate from the tree?

____

____

____

____

____

Now, read Genesis 3:3-9 again. What happened to the man and the woman in the garden? Did they die as we think of death?

____

____

____

____

____

Now let's look again at Deuteronomy 30:19-20, Who, does it say is our life?

____

____

____

____

____

My husband recently bought me the most beautiful bouquet of flowers. I quickly trimmed the stems and placed them in a vase full of water so that I could hopefully enjoy them as long as possible. As I walk by, I enjoy how the beautiful pops of color play off each other, and I sometimes lean over to smell their fragrance. I want to enjoy them as much as possible, as long as they last because as much as I hate to think about it, those flowers are dead. What I am enjoying is simply the life that is still left in them from when they were connected to their vine of origin. The moment they were cut from their original source, they ceased to live.

Now, as we go back to John 1:3-4, we see that our life, and light, our Original Vine, Our Source, Jesus, was coming into the world. And all the darkness of men could never stand against Him because He, alone holds life. **All of us together are like a bunch of flowers cut from a bush, we have no power to reconnect ourselves.** Yet, He was coming to become our Vine again, calling out to each one who is willing, "come, live again."

I want to finish by looking at our last verse in Mark 15:33. Write what Jesus is saying from the Cross, below.

____

____

____

____

____

Earlier in our lesson, we looked at Genesis 1:1 and talked about how the very first name of God was Elohim, Creator God, and that His name is plural and singular, meaning, "Mighty God." We also see in John 1 that Jesus was with God in the beginning, and that all things were made through Him, and that He was our Life, the Light of men.

Here at the Cross, we see a heartbreaking moment occurring between the Father and His only begotten Son, Jesus.

The One Who were always Three, now separate, for the first time ever. *"My God, My God,"* we became a *me*, the *our* became a *my*. **The lifegiving Vine was nailed to the lifeless tree.**

In the beginning, there was a forbidden tree, a man and a woman, and a garden where they walked naked and unashamed with God.

At the Cross, there was a tree, a man, hanging naked wearing our shame. The agony of the Cross all began in the Garden of Gethsemane, where Jesus would be led from to attach Himself fully to every sin that disattached us from Himself, and in so doing, reattached us back the only Vine that can give us Life.

"Yet it was the will of the LORD to crush him; he has put him to grief; when his soul shall make an offering for sin, he shall see his offspring and prolong his days; the will of the LORD shall prosper in his hand." (Isaiah 53:10)

The garden that was once sealed by flaming swords, for the first time became open by the Only One Who was able to walk back through the flaming swords of fire, and arise triumphant on the other side, paving a way of entry for each who would dare follow. The bride of Christ was born, her covering was secured at the Cross.

DAY 3

"I will greatly rejoice in the LORD; my soul shall exult in my God, for he has clothed me with the garments of salvation; he has covered me with the robe of righteousness, as a bridegroom decks himself, like a priests with a beautiful headdress, and a bride adorns herself with her jewels. For as the earth brings forth it's sprouts, and as a garden causes what is sown in it to sprout up, so the Lord God will cause righteousness and praise to sprout up before all the nations." (Isaiah 61:10-11)

"For everyone who does wicked things hates the light and does not come to the light, lest his deeds should be exposed. But whoever does what is true comes to the light so that it may be clearly seen that his deeds have been carried out by God." (John 3:21)

"And blessed is she who believed there would be a fulfillment of what was spoken to her from the LORD." (Luke 1:45)

Covering, it's what we all begin in, and seek out our whole lives journey. Like a hermit crab, there is something intrinsic to us that knows we can't survive without it. Every person has some sort of covering. Some find it in family, some in wealth or possessions, and some even in religion, social standing, or causes.

Jesus calls every other place we seek our covering outside of Him, *darkness*. It doesn't mean that these facets of our lives are all bad, it just means that we are never meant to find our refuge or identity in them.

Let's look at John 3:21 together and explore why, perhaps, Jesus wants our covering to be in Him alone.

Please, read the verse below as we examine the relationship that exists between God carrying us and us trying to carry ourselves. Record any thoughts you have below the scripture.

"For everyone who does wicked things hates the light and does not come to the light, lest his deeds should be exposed. But whoever does what is true comes to the light so that it may be clearly seen that his deeds have been carried out by God." (John 3:21)

What does God call what we do outside of abiding in His light?

____

____

____

____

____

This may seem rather harsh, yet when we compare it to the ancient Hebrew wedding, it sheds new *light* as we try to see things from God's perspective.

Remember that, when the second part of the wedding began, the *Nisuin*, or *Huppah* (meaning covering), the bride entered the bridal chamber where she was to stay for seven days, signifying her complete oneness with her bridegroom.

Remember also that the first part of the wedding, the *Kidisuin*, means Holy. In essence, the bride is saying, "my *I am* is in your *I am*, we are completely one." And even though she wasn't joined under the Huppah, or Covering, at that time (for the second part of the wedding had not yet occurred), she lived her whole life in light of that moment when she would be.

For her to suddenly not live her life as if she were one with her bridegroom meant she was taking herself out of his *I am*, it meant they were no longer one, or holy.

For her to place herself outside of her bridegroom would be unheard of because she didn't exist anymore outside of him. **For her to do that would mean that she had completely forgotten who she was. The bride doesn't make sense without the bridegroom.** We don't make sense in the dark because we have been brought into the light.

Let's explore an example of this as we look at Mary's story again. Meet me in Luke 1 as we read verses 39-56 together. Record any thoughts that stand out to you below.

____

____

____

____

____

What parts of this interchange point to Mary's acknowledgement that she has entered under the covering of Christ?

____

____

____

____

____

I don't know about you, but my heart is about to burst! This is one of the sweetest moments in scripture as two women, both experiencing a mixture of waiting and wonder and I imagine some fear of what others will think. Suddenly, they both burst-out with joy as the weight of what they are both carrying explodes under the weight of God's glory, as His very own Presence bursts from one swollen belly to the other, announcing, *"Arise and shine, for your light has come, and the glory of the LORD has risen upon you."* *(Isaiah 60:1).* The one who is providing covering to life Himself, is suddenly covered by His life bursting out through her. Whew, what a moment!

The words of Elizabeth under the inspiration of the Holy Spirt, are words that have carried me through much of my life's journey.

"And blessed is she who believed there would be a fulfillment of what was spoken to her from the LORD." (Luke 1:45)

Belief, it's our response to God's covering. Like the edge of His robe He lovingly holds open to us, our belief in Him is what moves us from merely acknowledging the robe is there to wrapping ourselves up in it.

Let's consider this concept further as we look at the scripture below.

"I will greatly rejoice in the LORD; my soul shall exult in my God, for he has clothed me with the garments of salvation; he has covered me with the robe of righteousness, as a bridegroom decks himself, like a priests with a beautiful headdress, and a bride adorns herself with her jewels. For as the earth brings forth it's sprouts, and as a garden causes what is sown in it to sprout up, so the Lord God will cause righteousness and praise to sprout up before all the nations." (Isaiah 61:10-11)

Underline every word that alludes to God covering us.

What does it say we are clothed in?

____

____

____

____

____

What does it say will sprout up before all the nations?

____

____

____

____

Do you believe God is causing this to happen for you? In what ways? If not, why not ask Him to show you how He wants to make this true about you.

____

____

____

____

____

As the two become One, under the covering, the Bridegroom at last covers His bride with who He fully is, who He fully is can't help but spring up out of the Bride. No matter where she is or what she faces, she is cloaked in Him, covered in His righteousness, and His salvation. Therefore, life, righteousness, and salvation sprout up through her, everywhere she goes.

She is the bride; she is His bride. They are one, at last.

"And blessed is she who believed there would be a fulfillment of what was spoken to her from the LORD." (Luke 1:45)

The word, **blessed**, in Hebrew is the word **barak**, it means, *to bow, to receive an inheritance, favor, praise, or honor.* In Hebrew, the words are read from right to left, opposite of how we read them, with each letter representing a small picture that ascribes meaning to what is being conveyed to the reader.

I want to close our lesson today by closely examining the meaning of the word, blessed, as I believe it perfectly portrays what happens when we enter God's covering through Jesus Christ, our Lord.

The first letter in bless is *beyt. Beyt* would be the start of the word bless, and it means; *house, tent, son, family, dwelling place, the physical tent/body, inside, within,* it's the first letter in the Torah that identifies the Son of God.

The scripture that comes to mind when I think of Beyt is John 10:9, *"I am the door. If anyone enters by me, he will be saved and will go in and out and find pasture."*

To help us "mark" this occasion and help us remember Jesus as our door to blessing, draw a door below.

The second letter in bless is *reysh*. *Reysh* is the middle letter in the word bless, *it means a person, the head, the highest, the sum, the supreme, the first, the most important, the top, master, leader, prince, head.*

The scripture that comes to mind when I think of *Reysh* is Matthew 22:37, "*And he said to him, "You shall love the LORD your God with all your heart, with all your soul and with all your mind."*

To help us "mark" this occasion and help us remember Jesus as our First, our King, and the One to Whom is due **all** *our worship, let's draw a picture of a crown in the space below.*

The third letter in bless is *kaf*. *Kaf* is the last letter in bless, it means; *to cover, to open, to allow, atonement, palm.*

The scripture that comes to mind when I think of kaf is John 3:16, "*For God so loved the world, that He gave His only Son, that whoever believes in him should not perish but have eternal life.*"

To help us "mark" this occasion and help us remember Jesus as our covering, the One Who held His palms open for us, as to give us the atonement of His own blood, draw a cross below.

When we truly look at the word bless, it becomes a word picture of Jesus, our **Door**, who literally nailed down our way to come back into perfect peace with our Father in heaven by meeting His demand that we love Him with all our heart, mind, soul and strength. The Father literally held out His open palms to us and gave the only thing that would hurt Him to give, in order to secure our way back home to His heart. We literally cannot separate the word bless from Jesus. He is our blessing and the source of all blessings that come to us.

Take a moment here to respond in any way you choose to this revelation of our Father's love for us.

____

____

____

____

____

Just to highlight what we are talking about here, let's go back to Genesis 2:28, the first time God blessed man and woman. *"And God blessed them. And God said to them. "Be fruitful and multiply and fill the earth and subdue it and have dominion over the fish of the sea and over the birds of the heavens and over every living thing that moves on the earth."*

Knowing now what blessing means, I hope you can see that man and woman were blessed because they were inside the Presence of God, they were physically and, in every way, living, moving and breathing in Him. **Just as the bride doesn't exist without the bridegroom, the blessings don't exist without the "Blesser".**

Therefore, when we read the devastating consequences that occurs due to man's fall, we see that the natural consequences of living life without the Blesser is a curse.

The blessing that was lost in the garden, is now being reconnected through the womb of a young Hebrew girl. A girl who is willing and ready to enter in to the tent God has opened to her to reconnect all who are willing to receive the atoning sacrifice of His Son, Jesus, the substance and source of every blessing.

DAY 4

"Thus, the heavens and the earth were finished, and all the hosts of them. And on the seventh day God finished his work that he had done, and he rested on the seventh day from all his work that he had done. So God blessed the seventh day and made it holy, because on it God rested from all his work that he had done in creation." (Genesis 2:1-3)

"Since it was the day of preparation, and so that the bodies would not remain on the cross on the Sabbath (for the Sabbath was a high day), the Jews asked Pilate that their legs might be broken and that they might be taken away." (John 19:31)

"Then the LORD said to Moses, 'Behold, I am about to rain bread from heaven for you, and the people shall go out and gather a day's portion every day, that I may test them, whether they will walk in my law or not. On the sixth day, when they prepare what they bring in, it will be twice as much as they gather daily.' (Exodus 16:4-5)

"Jesus said to them, 'I am the bread of life; whoever comes to me shall not hunger, and whoever believes in me shall never thirst.' (John 6:35)

As I prayed and asked Jesus how to end this study, He clearly directed me to end it as every wedding ends, with our eyes set on our new beginning. If you read the book's teaching portion of this series, you remember that there is a moment in the wedding when the bride emerges from the bridal chamber, unveiled for the first time, and proceeds to the covering of the Huppah with her husband where she makes seven circles around him. It marks one of the most moving and beautiful moments during the wedding. This is her openly showing the public, not who she will become, but who she's already become as the two are now one, the bride is now fully covered by her bridegroom, and her life fully revolves around him in every way. There is no longer a need for the veil because she is now covered fully in him. Any separation that existed between them has now ended; her whole life will be lived as an extension of this new beginning.

We will spend our last moments together embracing our new beginning as Christ's bride.

The number seven has great significance, not only in the Hebrew culture, but in the Bible. It represents God's completion, as well as His rest.

In the scripture below, circle each time the word rest, finished, or seven is mentioned.

"Thus, the heavens and the earth were finished, and all the hosts of them. And on the seventh day God finished his work that he had done, and he rested on the seventh day from all his work that he had done. So God blessed the seventh day and made it holy, because on it God rested from all his work that he had done in creation."(Genesis 2:1-3)

How many circles did you make?

____

____

____

____

____

The word for rest in Hebrew is *Shabath*, it is where the word, Sabbath comes from. It means; *to desists from exertion, to bring to an end, to rest, to silence, to still.*

The bride's circling portion of the ceremony reflects God's first creation of the world in 7 days, and how He created perfect order from nothing at all. Marriage, God's precious creation, in itself parallels God's working as He creates perfection where once there was nothing.

If we refer to the scripture above, what did God do on the seventh day?

____

____

____

____

____

Up until that point, did God call anything He had made Holy?

____

____

____

____

____

What does holy mean? How does this relate to a wedding?

____

____

____

____

____

That's right, if you remember, the first part of the wedding, the *Kidisuin*, is when the bridegroom veils his bride, and calls her, *"holy to me."* It means that she is set apart to him. She may still live in her father's home, but she is no longer part of that family.

So, a relationship exists between the seventh day, God's completion of His work, and rest. Let's explore this more as we look at scripture from Hebrews.

Let's read Hebrews 3:7-19 and answer the questions that follow.

What is the one thing God seeks after in His people? Is it our good works? Our sweet words? Our restless hearts that just want to do His will?

____

____

____

____

What is the relationship between disobedience, rest and unbelief?

____

____

____

____

In your opinion, what is the relationship between rest and blessing?

____

____

____

____

Today, we will examine how, as Christ's bride, we have the blessing of His rest. In fact, just as a Hebrew bride revolves around her bridegroom, we have the unique blessing and honor of revolving around Him from a place of rest.

We will examine some scriptures to help us understand this concept.

Let's begin from Exodus 16. I know it's long but read all of chapter 16. Record what stands out to you below, especially in reference to Sabbath and manna (bread from heaven).

____

____

____

____

____

There are so many references in the Old Testament to the number 7 and how it relates to both the completion of God's judgement or His blessings on His people and I encourage you, as you read your Bible to pay attention to such details as they all point to His faithfulness towards us. I chose to use this example because it so clearly points to Jesus, our heavenly Manna, and Bridegroom, and how He gives us rest.

Did the children of Israel seem to be at rest? What indications lead us to believe they were not?

____

____

____

____

____

In verse 4 how does God say He is going to handle the situation?

____

____

____

____

____

In verse 5, what specific instructions are given about the 6th day?

____

____

____

____

____

In verses 22-26, how does God exhibit His provision for His people so that they may have rest?

____

____

____

____

____

God provided a double portion on the 6th day so that His people could experience the blessing on 7th day rest. The amazing thing about the manna is that it spoiled every other day when the Israelites tried to keep it over for the next day. Only when God provided the 6th day manna, did is supernaturally maintain its freshness.

Just as the number 7 is a special number in the Bible, so is the number 6. In the Bible, the number 6 represents man, for man was made on the 6th day. This is important as we now look at the timing of what took place in the New Testament, when our Bridegroom faithfully came for us, giving every reason to trust in the rest that He, alone, can provide.

Let's jump over to John 6 and read verses 22-40. After reading these verses, record any correlation to Jesus' words and how they relate to what we read above.

____

____

____

____

Does Jesus refer to Himself as our heavenly manna in these verses?

____

____

____

____

Now, let's jump over to John 19 and read verses 28-31. According to these verses, Jesus, our Manna from heaven did what? And on what day?

____

____

____

____

I hope you caught this, my precious sisters, because there is such **rest** and **assurance** packed in this precious knowledge. Like the thin red string tied to Rahab's window, ensuring her that she and her family could have hope, even when every wall around them was falling down, these verses string together an assurance in our hearts that, once let in, will hold us up and give us a supernatural rest that comes straight from Jesus, our Manna from heaven.

According to theses verses, let's draw and label a timeline below that explains what happened. Here are the terms to use in your timeline.

(6th day (day of preparation), Cross , Jesus, 7th day (Sabbath)).

"Since it was the day of Preparation, and so that the bodies would not remain on the cross on the Sabbath (for the Sabbath was a high day), the Jews asked Pilate that their legs might be broken and that they might be taken away." (John 19:31)

The 6th day, the day of man, Jesus died for man. This was the day of preparation, the day when we are to go collect our double portion so that we have ample provision for the Sabbath, our time for blessed rest.

The 7th day, Jesus, our Bread from heaven, rested from all His works, just as His Father had done at the creation.

Our Bridegroom, Jesus, rested and in so doing, extends the rest of His double portion to us, His bride. The bride gets to encircle her Bridegroom because her completion and rest, all her sevens, are found in Him alone.

Let's look closely into the relationship between our rest and our obedience.

Let's read Hebrews 3:7-4:9. Record any thoughts or insights to these scriptures below.

____

____

____

____

____

Hebrews 4:3 is amazing and, like a bookend, points right back to Genesis 2:3 where it says, *"So God blessed the seventh day and made it holy, because on it God rested from all his work that he had done in creation."* God's perfect and complete provision for us was made, and there is literally nothing left for us to do, but to believe in **all** He did for us. As Ephesians 1:4 assures us, *"even as he chose us in him before the foundation of the world, that we should be holy and blameless before him in love".* There is nothing sweeter to our Father's heart than a believing bride, a bride that gets up every morning ready to taste and see that her Bridegroom is good and His provisions for her are sure. Even if the whole world is crumbling around her, she is standing firm in the One Who cannot, and will never leave her disappointed, for He has rested her in His love. All her *I am's* are in Him, and in Him alone.

DAY 5

"Soon afterward he went on through cities and villages, proclaiming and bringing the good news of the kingdom of God. And the twelve were with him, and also some women who had been healed of evil spirits and infirmities: Mary, called Magdalene, from whom seven demons had gone out, and Joanna, the wife of Chuza, Herod's household manager, and Susanna, and many others, who provided for them out of their means." (Luke 8:1-3)

"At this, she turned around and saw Jesus standing there, but she did not realize that it was Jesus. He asked her, "Woman, why are you crying? Who is it you are looking for? Thinking he was the gardener, she said, 'Sir, if you have carried him away, tell me where you have put him, and I will get him.'

Jesus said to her, 'Mary'

She turned toward him and cried out in Aramaic, 'Rabboni!' (which means 'Teacher'). Jesus said, 'Do not hold on to me, for I have not yet ascended to the Father. Go instead to my brothers and tell them, 'I am ascending to my Father and your Father, to my God and your God." (John 20:14-17)

I am in awe of God's timing and perfection, both in His Word and in His sovereignty in our lives. As I sit here writing our final day of study, outside my door are the sounds of painters and craftsmen, sealing up the final touches in our home from where an improper covering (our weak roof) left our home damaged within. As I mentioned at the beginning of this week's lesson, we all seek covering, but there is only one covering that is all sufficient. We will spend our last day together with Mary Magdelene, our perfect case study of a woman who knew how to simply abide in Christ's covering.

Let's get to know Mary as we read the scriptures below and reflect on what Jesus meant to her.

"Soon afterward he went on through cities and villages, proclaiming and bringing the good news of the kingdom of God. And the twelve were with him, and also some women who had been healed of evil spirits and infirmities: Mary, called Magdalene, from whom seven demons had gone out, and Joanna, the wife of Chuza, Herod's household manager, and Susanna, and many others, who provided for them out of their means." (Luke 8:1-3)

First, how many evil spirits were cast out of Mary?

____

____

____

____

____

Secondly, what does it say these women were doing?

____

____

____

____

____

My mind was blown when I first realized that Jesus' earthly ministry was in large part financed by women who were blessed by His ministry. As someone who is led to serve in ministry, and have felt the tug between the desire to serve the Lord and the tangible cost of doing so, it blessed my heart and opened my eyes to see Jesus perfectly demonstrating humility even in how He received financial support for His ministry. The One who could have continually pulled coins from fishes' mouths, or caused bread to fall from heaven, instead chose to use His need for earthly means as a way to exalt those who were often looked down upon and overlooked. From the beginning, our Covering, Jesus, was demonstrating what it looks like to cover one another.

"If I then, your LORD, and Teacher, have washed your feet, you also ought to wash one another's feet. For I have given you an example, that you also should do just as I have done to you. Truly, truly I say to you, a servant is not greater than his master, nor is a

messenger greater than the one who sent him. If you know these things, blessed are you if you do them." (John 13:14-16)

It makes me chuckle to think of how the wisdom of God played out through Jesus' ministry. From the beginning, Jesus was teaching His followers the beauty of how His love covers us all and makes us all equal at His feet. I can't imagine the early male disciples getting away with holding divisive opinions about women, when they were the ones literally buttering the bread, they ate. And the women could see the wisdom of God as they watched men who had once regarded them as property, suddenly see them as sisters, and co-heirs with Christ. **A blessed interdependence was born out of love for God, and a need for one another to accomplish together through God, what they could never do on their own.** Two became one, held together in the perfect love of Jesus Christ.

"...and they shall become one flesh. And they were both naked and not ashamed." (Gen. 2:24b-25)

Sometimes, we confuse our desire to cover Christ (or what we perceive as Him) with His desire to cover us. One covering leads to striving while the other leads to rest. **Have you ever experienced any confusion between the two?** Boy, I know I have! This is one of those moments I wish we were sitting down across a cozy table with two cups of coffee, to compare stories and maybe shed a few frustrated tears together.

Grab your coffee and sit with me as you share in the space below.

Where have you struggled most with trying to cover Christ as opposed to letting Him cover you?

Name what keeps you from entering the covering of His rest, write it below and explain.

As a girl who grew up without the covering of an earthly father, I know what it is to live under the oppressing weight of insecurity and loss of safety. I rarely felt safe as a child and experienced many consequences of not being properly covered. That sense of insecurity spilled into my adult life and wrecked whatever decision could have led me towards covering. Those of us who grew up without a covering wrongly assume it's up to us to make our own covering. But how can we? **Every attempt I made to cover myself led me deeper and deeper into self-destruction.**

One day, just like Mary Magdalene, I met my *seven*. In the bible the number seven represents completion. It can be amazing in the context of "it is finished" and totally devastating when it means "I am finished". Mine was the latter. I was done with me!

I didn't even trust myself to make one more decision and all my prior choices were haunting me, like Mary's seven demons. I was a single mom at the time and pregnant with my second child. I had just left an abusive marriage and was seeing the full manifestation of my self-sufficiency, my attempts to find my own covering, manifested themselves in an overwhelming mountain of pain neither I nor my children could bear. There was no escape from it.

This was the moment I first turned to Jesus for covering.

I had received Him, or so I thought, earlier in my life, but I did not know how to need Him.

I didn't really trust that He was real enough for me to seek refuge in.

I didn't discover that until, like a scared and abused kitten fleeing the storm, I ran into the arms of Jesus and suddenly discovered there was a covering there, waiting for me the whole time.

I exchanged my seven of Rhonda's defective and incomplete self-covering for the seven of Christ's sufficient and complete covering. And in doing so, I found rest. True rest. **The kind that only comes when one is completely covered from head to toe with love.**

I found my covering in Christ alone.

After reading those words, you might think I had it down after coming to Jesus. I didn't.

I knew I had found what sufficient covering looked like, but I had no idea how to stay in it. Like the Israelite's who were suddenly freed by God when Moses came to rescue them from Egypt, I knew I was suddenly in a whole new domain that was where I had always wanted to be, but almost as quickly as I got there, my own propensity to try and manage what I had just received threaten to leave me from experiencing the REST and JOY it had covered me in.

Inside of me, I still carried a deep sense of insecurity that left me feeling as if I had to earn my covering to ensure that I would never lose it. **How does one suddenly understand how-to live-in grace, which by definition, is something that is completely undeserved?**

This is why I love Mary Magdelene and her interaction with Jesus in John 20 so much.

"At this, she turned around and saw Jesus standing there, but she did not realize that it was Jesus. He asked her, "Woman, why are you crying? Who is it you are looking for?

Thinking he was the gardener, she said, 'Sir, if you have carried him away, tell me where you have put him, and I will get him.'

Jesus said to her, 'Mary'

She turned toward him and cried out in Aramaic, 'Rabboni!' (which means 'Teacher'). Jesus said, 'Do not hold on to me, for I have not yet ascended to the Father. Go instead to my brothers and tell them, 'I am ascending to my Father and your Father, to my God and your God." (John 20:14-17)

In order to better understand where Mary was coming from, let's go back and read a little bit more about Mary's experiences. Meet me in the scriptures below and record any significant information you find about Mary.

Matthew 27:56, 61

____

____

____

____

____

Matthew 28:1

____

____

____

____

____

Mark 16:1-19

We can ascertain from scripture that not only did Mary become a disciple and sup-porter of Jesus' ministry after He delivered her, but she was also one of the few who served Him to the end.

After all, where else could she go? He was the one who had delivered her from her seven. Not only that, He had become her Seven, *her completion*. Scripture records that she had followed Jesus all the way to the Cross, and even watched where He was laid. She had lived her life in gratitude to Him. And now that He was gone, she would con-tinue serving Him or what was left of Him. Perhaps, like me, she lived in such a deep sense of gratitude for what Christ had done for her that her service back to Him was the least she could do. In a sense, it was her way of offering the only covering she had left to give, that of giving back to Him what He had given to her.

Matthew 28:1 marked the beginning of a brand new day for her, as well as for each one of us who will embrace it. *"Now after the Sabbath the first day of the week began to dawn, Mary Magdelene, and the other Mary came to the tomb."*

"Therefore if anyone is in Christ, he is a new creation. The old has passed away; behold, the new has come." (2 Corinthians 5:17)

Yesterday, we talked about the 7th day and how Jesus rested. Guess what happened after that?

He woke up!

And guess what happened after that?

He invites us all to wake up with Him, beginning with, you guessed it, Mary!

He reaches out to Mary and becomes to her the very expression of Himself when He said in Isaiah 60:1, *"Arise, shine, for your light has come! And the glory of the LORD is risen on you."*

For the first time since the garden of Eden, man was invited to walk in God's perfect light, and extending His Light to all who will come and acknowledge their desire to rise in it. Christ and His Bride are one at last. All her sevens are complete in Him. **The last seven, death, has finally been completed. The old had passed away and a brand-new day had dawned for Mary and for us, the Church, the bride of Christ.**

As Mary reaches out to cling to Jesus, perhaps, Jesus saw in her a propensity to relate to Him according to her old way, to the way she had before the Cross, before the resurrection. He tells her, *"Do not hold on to me, for I have not yet ascended to the Father. Go instead to my brothers and tell them, 'I am ascending to my Father and your Father, to my God and your God."* (John 20:17) Mary, the woman who had served Jesus, loved Jesus, and walked beside Jesus, was going to have to learn to relate to Him in a whole new way. Yes, even Mary had to, *"strive to enter the rest"* that was now made available to her. The Jesus who had been her healer, her teacher, and her friend, had now become her Savior and King. Her teacher had become her Bridegroom and she had become His bride, a whole new creation! The extension of God's robe as held out over Mary; her perfect covering had come.

The darkest ending of all time had erupted with the brightest dawn of all time, a new day had arrived, a chance for Christ's bride to stand beside Him, perfectly reflecting the glory of all God had created from the very beginning.

"Therefore a man shall leave his father and mother and be joined to his wife and they shall become one flesh." (Genesis 2:24)

Bride, listen closely and you will hear who you are, who you became as Christ's bride. The world can become really loud, yet the new creation you became in Christ is stronger and has overcome the whole world.

Your oneness with Christ calls out within you, from under His covering, beckoning all around you who are thirsty, lost, broken, and hurting to come in, to come and be made new and whole as the bride of Christ. Your story is waiting to begin, and it's the greatest love story ever told.

"I, Jesus, have sent My angel to testify about these things in the churches. I am the Root and the Offspring of David, the Bright and Morning Star.

And the Spirit and the bride say, "Come!" And let him who hears say, "Come!" And let him who is thirsty come. Whoever desires, let him take the water of life freely." (Revelation 22:16-17)